Charisma

Charisma

a psychoanalytic look at mass society

Irvine Schiffer MD

FACULTY OF THE CANADIAN INSTITUTE OF PSYCHOANALYSIS

RESEARCH PROFESSOR OF POLITICAL ECONOMY AND

ASSOCIATE PROFESSOR OF PSYCHIATRY, UNIVERSITY OF TORONTO

University of Toronto Press

Especially for Ellen, Susan and Marc, Laura and David

Contents

Introduction

This study attempts to cover a wide range of charismatic phenomena, but it dwells in particular on certain abstractions in our individual and collective psychologies that operate in the imaging of emotionally laden figures and that can find their ultimate expression in our choice of a political leader. Since it attempts to throw light on some determinants of people's political reactions, I could describe this book as a treatise on psychic epidemiology: the 'organism' I try to isolate is that particular condition of man which promotes and fashions a design for leadership, a design whose style has been cyclical, recurrent, and unchanging down through the years.

A Freudian psychoanalyst by profession, I offer here some thoughts that have been shaped, naturally enough, by the yeast of mainstream thinking in this field. Yet my central thesis does not echo the more speculative Freudian psychology dealing with groups any more than it reflects the traditional teachings of other established institutions in this field. Although I desire my own free voice, I rely for the legitimacy of my concepts on my clinical experiences and on the corroborative support of my colleagues in the communal world of psychological skill.

One of my aims in this book is to dramatize the significance of the masses in the choice of political leaders, despite the common tendency in our culture to see such leaders and experts as self-made men. There is barely an area in our daily life untouched by authorities of one kind or another, instructing us on the use of both mind and body; we are subsumed by an army of specialists, hired to protect us from the hardening of our arteries and the softening of our minds. Even our sexual aberrations have been taken out of the realm of the private by social scientists; pornography has become the new 'sexology'.

But there is one area of our life where we, the people, should logically be the experts. That is the field of politics. In our democracies, we like to think that we, the masses, are in control of our political life, that we require to be neither advised nor instructed on how we should vote. Yet there are those 'professional' manipulators of public opinion who ply us with stimuli, watching ever so closely for our reactions, constantly on the look-out for indicators of our tastes, our habits, and our preferences on a wide range of issues pertaining to the public character. When such skilled personnel spend years of research into the political habits of people, they manage to collect an impressive amount of information on the voting patterns and political receptivities of a nation. The result is that the manipulators in the service of the parties are armed with much more knowledge about us than we have of our own psychology and behaviour.

This situation is undesirable. I have made some effort to investigate and understand electoral behaviour, and I publish my observations in the service of insight and democracy rather than of instruction and manipulation. It is an aim of this study to contribute to self-education in a focal area which might be called the psycho-politics of people — an area that derives its significance from something beyond traditional socio-political concerns.

I am hopeful that, though the reader will recognize my reliance on Freudian psychology, most notably on the writings of the master himself, he will also discover, interspersed throughout this work, the skein of an original thesis drawn in large measure from clinical observations I have compiled during my day-to-day consultations with people from different walks of life. In brief, my study aims to demonstrate how each individual in a society contributes his own unique developmental conflicts and his own heroic imagery to the creation of that communal idealized image of man — the charismatic leader. Accordingly, I try to reveal those salient features of our individual personalities and character structures as these relate to the adaptation we make within our political society.

I should like to acknowledge the assistance of those psychologists and social scientists whose works form the substance of my bibliographic references. I wish also to express my indebtedness to R.I.K. Davidson of the editorial staff of the University of Toronto Press, whose assistance and many helpful suggestions have so facilitated the preparation of this book.

Some
psychological
terms

I

Self or *identity:* an abstraction within the mind, composed of largely conscious mental images which have to do with our social interaction with others and with the outside world in general

Ego identity: the identity which approximates the particular niche in society which is compatible with one's expectations and self-respect (Erikson)

Narcissism: the investment of the self with libido (cathexis of the self)

Rescue of narcissism: the techniques one employs in safeguarding against a diminution or depletion of one's narcissistic self-esteem

Omnipotence: the illusion of being all-powerful; a stage in the psychic evolution of the child wherein his infantile narcissism allows him the illusion of his being more powerful than he is

II

Symbiosis: a psychological fusional state wherein the self and the object appear both dependent on each other, as if they were one

Individuation: a process of psychological separation between self and an object; the opposite to symbiosis

Conversion: a psychological shunting or displacement of instinctual charge from a mental experience to a physical or bodily experience

III PSYCHIC COMPLEXES

Oedipus complex: an instinctually charged rivalry between father and son, or between mother and daughter

Negative oedipus complex: rivalry between father and daughter or between mother and son

Castration complex: an anxiety emanating from a fear (usually fantasied) of punishment, as anticipated from the parent who is one's rival in the oedipus complex

Family romance: a complex emerging within the developing conscience and characterized by the idealization of extra-familial objects; the romance stage of an individual denotes a stage in the evolution of his idealizations when he conceives his family romance; it is characterized by heroic fantasies of an especially aggressive nature that become projected onto outside leaders

IV   THE THREE AGENCIES OF THE PSYCHIC APPARATUS

Instinct (or *id*): aggression and libido
Ego: the executive agency of the psyche that adjusts, synthesizes, discriminates, and mediates between instinct and inner as well as outer reality
Conscience (*superego* and/or *ego ideal*): a judging and evaluating agency that embraces, criticizes, and polices one's ideals; superego is the punitive conscience, ego ideal the forgiving and reconciling conscience

V   THE DEFENCE MECHANISMS OF THE PSYCHIC APPARATUS
germane to this thesis

Projection: the psychic process whereby the individual perceives his own psychological machinations as originating from outside himself; it is instrumental in the development of one's sense of reality
Incorporation: the psychic process in which the individual perceives the psychological machinations of others as originating from inside himself; it is also instrumental in the development of one's sense of reality
Repression: a mechanism which banishes that which is conscious to a state of unconsciousness; an example is forgetting
Dissociation: a splitting within the ego that allows (unsuccessfully) for an unwanted fragment of one's psychic motivations to become compartmentalized and disowned; a real or threatened breakdown in this mechanism commonly forces the ego then to project the disowned fragment onto some external object
Rescue: a technique of the ego as well as a phenomenon of conscience wherein self-esteem is restored or maintained, i.e., rescue of narcissism; it is synonymous with *rescue operation* (as in charismatic rescue operation)

Charisma

Chapter 1

The projected image

From time to time in history, there has appeared a phenomenon with the unique ingredients of mob psychology. It springs up as if from nowhere and proceeds on a broad sweeping course through a group, with each passing day gaining the reinforcement of a citizenry involuntarily caught up in the process like the victims of a strange disease. The earliest symptoms of such epidemics are often far from clear in the minds of historians attempting to document their onset. Commonly, the provocative agent is identified as being some specific individual, whose unique personality is supposedly the true source of the process; but at other times, the individual is seen as only a standard-bearer for a new and exciting ideology. It may be a person or it may be a cause that is held responsible for stirring up the communal empathy of a people. As the wave gains momentum, the media of communication — once bards, now TV cameras and commentators — may lend a lustre and dimension to the whole happening; a strange hypnoid state begins to infiltrate the most vulnerable minds. In our day, the social scientist looks for economic and cultural factors as he tries to explain the new 'miracle'; the intelligentsia dissect the personal mystique of the hero; avant-garde theories and sophisticated clichés bombard the mind, already softened by the media's propaganda. Like a rash in a communicable disease, the first reaction develops into a deeper and fevered agitation gripping the body politic. The disease takes full hold, and many parts of society succumb to a strange and crippling affliction: charisma.

Max Weber (1922) offered the first conceptualization of the term charisma (borrowed from Rudolph Sohn), which he defined as an exceptional quality in an individual who, through appearing to possess supernatural, providential, or extraordinary powers, succeeds in gathering disciples around him. Though Weber's writings acknowledge in some degree the importance of group psychology to the charismatic personality, they give little attention to any specific dynamism operative in the group; rather they portray the disciples as blind followers, totally captivated by the forceful magnetism of their leader. Though Weber's idea of charisma required there to be a crowd of followers, the crowd had little psychological significance other than in the relation between the individual members and the one who commanded their devotion.

Weber derived his understanding of charisma mainly from his study of the salvation religions which, being at the service of sacred convictions rather than of laws, he viewed as most prone to functioning in a revolutionary manner through the elements of charismatic prophecy which sustained them. Religions could raise the bearer of charisma to a mystical level where he became a prophet, entitled to speak for a god. In contrast to the priest, Weber's prophet carried a personal aura of 'break-through'; unlike the magician, he was a sorcerer with an innovative aura and a personal magnetic gift, but he promoted a specific doctrine.

In describing his man of charisma as a mystical ascetic, concerned with himself rather than involved with others, Weber showed an intuitive awareness of the significant element of narcissism in the phenomenon. He recognized that there was something beyond material gain operative in one exercising charismatic influence; an idea was promoted for its own sake, without motive of gain or worldly profit. When it occurred in politics, Weber's charismatic authority held an exceptional type of power: it set aside the usages of normal political life and assumed instead those of demagoguery, dictatorship, or revolution. Such usages, activities, and roles he perceived as inducing men's whole-hearted devotion to the charismatic individual through a blind and fanatical trust and an unrestrained and uncritical faith.

A key quality in Weber's description of charisma was a break with continuity. There was a challenge to the established order, constructive and at the same time destructive, where boundaries were established by someone drawing his legitimacy only from sources within himself. Weber perceived the influence of such a leader as in direct proportion to the distance he placed between himself and any political affiliation. Weberian charismatic policy represented an adventure, not only because it courted failure but because it was constantly obliged to discover a new impetus for enthusiasm, one that could tear men from boredom and exalt the more inspirational aspects of life. Weber astutely observed that, though theoretically the horizons for the charismatic leader were unlimited, yet when doubt assailed the followers the power was doomed to collapse. Weber concluded that the basic problem of such authority was one of succession: who could take over after the demise of a leader whose charisma could be neither learned nor taught, only aroused and experienced? In substance, charismatic leadership was characterized by a lack of continuity, by movement rather than stability, and by a disregard for public opinion. Such leadership was a calling that transcended democratic representation.

Since Weber, sociologists and historians such as Talcott Parsons (1967) and Arthur Schlesinger Jr (1960) have questioned his concept. They have noted that his classification of political leaderships — traditional, rational, and charismatic — hardly applies to present-day democracies where power or authority is no longer seen to be simply one or other of these three types, though the governing of such democracies may well display any or all three of these qualities in leadership. Schlesinger, quite articulate in this direction, has argued that in modern society there exists a practical dominance of forces, personality appeals, and policies that leaves no room whatever for charisma, because charisma is basically incapable of dealing with the realities of a democratic culture. He conceded that the charisma of Hitler was of vital significance to the ascendancy of the Third Reich, where irrationality ascribed to divine influence was the order of the day. But he suggested further that certain political figures carrying some personal ordainment of personality, which for Schlesinger was apparently innately charismatic, had an obligation in time of crisis to rise above others in keeping with their greatness. Though he felt that to use the concept of charisma to explain any conscious organizational leadership of today would be futile, he admitted, paradoxically, that democratic theory remains baffled about leadership in general and is unprepared to explain the necessities of heroic leadership within a democratic structure. He saw laws and government as machinery transcending the cult of personality, and he recognized the significance of appropriate institutions that allowed the instructed few to disseminate insights to the many. Yet among those institutions are the various psychoanalytic societies which, for me, hold the most promise of educating the people about the unconscious machinations that play a role in directing popular choice; and these Schlesinger has castigated as 'eliminators of complexes' who would have modern society take flight from hero worship and dispense with the 'great man'. His own somewhat concealed heroic ideals show through also in his support of the idea that charges the heroic leader with the Promethean responsibility of securing a human freedom against the supposed inevitabilities of history. For Schlesinger then, there is still a place for heroic leadership in our times; despite its complexion of sober democratic realism, his thought is coloured with an elitist psychology that justifies the very cult of personality it ostensibly deplores.

The one surprising feature of his concepts is an unpreparedness to recognize what is, for me, a significant psychological factor in leadership — namely, that all leaders, including the charismatic, are to a meaningful degree creations of the people. The elitism of Schlesinger, as of Weber, allows the image of greatness to appear as prompted by some unique capacity or calling emanating from within the leader himself.

Further, I take issue with the view that democracy today, either in its theory or its practice, prevents the phenomenon of charisma. There is no evidence that the wheels of democracy are busily churning for the enlightenment of a society that might select leaders who transcend the glamour of the charismatic. As I see it, our democratic nations are still heavily tainted with both hero-worshippers and iconoclasts; their vociferous numbers bear testimony to the fact that our leaderships do not yet provide any facilitation for the people's initiating and decision-making capacities. As is painfully obvious, especially in time of crisis, people who have seen fit to begin by blaming everything on their leader end by confirming their original willingness to let him do it all.

I suggest that charisma lives on and continues to play, as it has in the past, that subtly seductive and at times infantilizing role in today's democratic processes. The concept has undergone major variations since it was noted and defined by Weber, but the emotional elements of charisma are still very much the same; they are as dynamically alive in the mass psyche of today as in that of yesteryear, as latent and ready to be activated as they were thirty, three hundred, or three thousand years ago. Schlesinger's complacent conviction notwithstanding, the apparatus of stable government has not pushed into obsolescence all those irrational forces that promote charismatic leadership. As I see it, such forces rest neither in their entirety nor even predominately within the personality of our leaders: rather they depend on the standards of education of people at large and on the degree to which such irrational forces express the fluctuating moods and sensitivities of an inherently ambivalent humanity. Nor can I share Schlesinger's romanticism that finds his hero realized among the chosen few: the hero (or heroine) is an intrinsic universal image of every individual at one or another stage in personal development, an omnipotent and sometimes pathetically quixotic cavalier that insists on pervading the minds of both those who live primarily within themselves and those caught up more actively in the affairs of their country. Charisma, especially in the field of politics, is with us still.

Weber referred to a state of society ready to deviate from a normative order, and his concept of break-through involved a culture ready for revolutionary change, a culture sensitized and predisposed to such change by the forceful leadership of a charismatic prophet. He described such preparedness in society as its 'alienation potential', a potential heightened by any influence that weakened traditionalism in the established order. He felt that the intellectualization of relatively non-privileged groups outside the main prestige structure of a society played a key role in its being so sensitized, but that, by and large, the masses made no greater contribution than passive receptivity toward the emergence of the charismatic leader. The ultimate locus of charisma he placed full on the shoulders of the individual who possessed it, who by his very essence commanded it. Weber's concept seems an over-simplification; for surely in every period of man's history figures have emerged from various ranks of society and reaped, at least temporarily, a public acclaim; and there is no plausible evidence that such leadership was dictated by forces lying either in their personalities or their expressed ideologies.

I do not deny that there have been many charismatic leaders who have earned their public identification from something more than the collective imagery of a following: Martin Luther and his religious manifesto, Hitler and his racist ideology, Abraham Lincoln and his emancipation of the American Slaves — such men gained leadership largely through their personalities and ideologies. Yet I think it neither frivolous nor cynical to suggest that, even now, as throughout the ages, the people of all nations have not in the main been equipped with insight and comprehension into the socio-cultural and economic forces of their time. It is not naive to contend that there are vast masses of people in our democratic societies who are still totally indifferent to or ignorant of the public affairs of their own nation and of international affairs as well. It is not far-fetched to hypothesize then, that individual choices for national leadership might in many instances rest not on an individual's interests or knowl-edge of the times but rather on more deep-rooted, highly personalized passions that are linked with the everyday psycho-logical imagery that people harbour within themselves — an imagery that stems from the influences of their earliest years.

To a large number of people (the proportion in a given society would be purely speculative) political figures may well represent little more than names and images. They are just like box-office attractions in the field of entertainment — this despite the fact that many politicians are often bearers of ideals and ideologies. It is incontestable that our culture continues to embrace the images of certain internationally popular actors, actresses, and musicians who, above and beyond their talents, have been given charismatic status despite — or perhaps because of — certain flaws in their character or theatrical skills. Many such figures have been taken into the hearts of the masses as the result of a complex combination of factors that relate to group psychological processes. Among these processes one must include the individual and communal imagery of mankind, an imagery whose solipsistic content people strive so endlessly to project onto some outside figure, in order to bring to fruition the fulfilment — vicarious though it may be — of their own creative ambitions for themselves.

Moralists might discount imaging individuals as deplorably superficial. I hope to illustrate in this study that people basically under the sway of their imagery are by no means simpletons in a psychological sense. The psyche of an individual, regardless of his political or cultural naïvetés, is a most complex mechanism, and the capacity for imagery has its roots in as yet unfathomed depths of the human mind. The psychic functioning of those fixated at the level of imagery is more predominantly under the sway of very personalized individual forces and is therefore capable of reinforcement by any mob influence. Regression to imagery even in intelligent adults is not only one of the prime symptoms of mob regression, but is also a state of mind that occurs in every individual on many occasions in his or her life, such as when fatigue sets in or when one is at play or succumbing to excessive emotional stress. Rather than pass judgment on those with a special predilection for making political choices and decisions based on imagery, I prefer to reappraise the forces

that perpetuate the images, the passions, and the romanticisms that have always attached themselves to political
leadership.

I am arguing in this book that large numbers of people,
though they may be relatively realistic in their personal lives,
do in fact still select their public leaders predominantly on
the basis of imagery. Such imaging people have the capacity
to reject or to glamorize – even to deify – a political leader,
while having about the same level of comprehension about
that leader as they might have for a popular entertainer.
Many imaging people in many instances can and do allow
their idiosyncratic tastes and preferences to over-ride completely whatever relates to reasoning and the political realities. Just as these tastes can and do lead to charismatic
acknowledgment of some unwholesome people in the field
of entertainment, so they have allowed, from time to time in
world events, some of the strange paradoxes in mass behaviour that have given a frightening mandate to despotism
and tyranny.

I am not saying, of course, that the leaders famous in
world history were psychological monsters any more than I
am suggesting that they were colourless blobs, whimsically
and randomly chosen to play out the communal fancies of a
people. On the contrary, people *en masse* have responded to
the remarkable capacities of many leaders, some of whom
possessed a rare courage, others who awesomely inspired a
people's ethics, and still others who harboured a special gift
for inciting a people to hate, violence, and even self-
destruction. What I am saying is that, without the initial
free-floating creative thrust of a people at large, perhaps some
of the most brilliant as well as some of the most malignant of
public figures of any era might never have risen so high or
reaped the harvest of their particular charismatic qualities. I
make the further contention that certain individuals, not
particularly blessed with either special skills or significant
ideologies, have received, under certain conditions of human
crisis, a call to the charismatic role. Such a call has not simply

emanated from an intrinsic inspirational force within their individual personalities, but came as well from a rescue-hungry people, prepared in their distress to invest a leader with charisma.

THE PROJECTIVE WAY OF LIFE

In my approach to the psychological factors involved in political leadership in general and in charismatic leadership in particular, the student of philosophy may recognize thoughts reminiscent of the pre-Freudian dilemmas of men such as Kant and Schopenhauer. The classical philosophical investigation of the origin, structure, validity, and methods of ascertaining knowledge about human phenomena concerned itself primarily with the psychology of the subject who views the phenomenon and not the phenomenon itself. In this study the subject and the phenomenon are two aspects of the same thing.

In philosophic circles such a position will no doubt be labelled one of 'rationalism', in opposition to the 'empiricist' approach which identifies the sole source of knowledge as experience. Where the empiricist views the human being as primarily dependent upon his environment and the stimulations coming from it, the extreme rationalist tends to reduce all objects to existing solely in his own subjective world of reason. Schopenhauer pronounced that 'the world is my idea ... what [a man] knows is not a sun and an earth, but only an eye that sees a sun and feels an earth; the world which surrounds him is there only as idea, i.e., only in relation to something else, the consciousness which is himself.' For Schopenhauer, all that existed was only object in relation to subject, the perception of a perceiver — 'in a word, idea.'

In contrast to such solipsism, Kant had earlier set out the path of reconciliation between the extreme rationalist and the equally extreme empiricist. Among the latter, Hume, for example, maintained that reasoning involved in studying subjective ideas was but a mere dabbling in illusion. As the father of pragmatic philosophy, Hume argued that the basis of our knowledge of the world was the law of probabilities — an estimate of the likelihood for the recurrence of events based on the frequency of the sequential appearances of such phenomena. Kant's efforts to bridge the gap between solipsism and pragmatism led to his own brand of dynamic psychology where he explored and analysed the interrelationship of the individual and his environment, attempting to do justice to both as significant. It could be said of Kant that he was one of several who led the way to Freud's views on dynamic psychology. Kant made a sharp cleavage between our 'sensibility' (or what we would call today perception) on the one hand and the 'thing in itself' (the real world about which we know nothing directly but only through our perception). Kant saw pure rationalist philosophy as dealing with possible experience, nothing more in effect than mere appearances; he felt that the understanding of such appearances did not derive its laws 'from' nature but prescribed them 'to' nature. He recognized that in our minds we have principles according to which incoming stimulation is organized and interpreted, thereby becoming converted into experience. In contrast to Hume's 'random probabilities' as a view of the world, Kant saw a universe which, owing to the existence of the human mind, was ordered and amenable to systematic exploration.

This philosophical recapitulation is intended to illuminate further the course this volume aims to take, not only in relationship to psychology as we know it today, but also as it relates to those speculative systems that have laid the groundwork for the present-day philosopher's view of man's perception of man. Though my approach at first look may bear some remote resemblance to Schopenhauer's philosophy, the topic of leadership will of necessity be approached from two sides in an effort to reach my own reconciliatory position. From one side, emphasized in this volume, I examine the role of the psychology of the subject, in this instance the people, their creative processes, and their perceptions that condition their ultimate choice of leaderships. But there will follow a separate book in which the role of the personality and character of individual political figures will be appraised, in terms of the capacities of these leaders to stimulate, as well as to modify, the over-all psychology of the masses.

Lest the reader protest that such a double-pronged approach splits what is basically one merged process, let me state that my choice has been prompted purely by a practical consideration, namely, simplicity. The totality of the psychology of leadership is immensely complex and intricate: one need only imagine trying to make a comprehensive assessment, for example, of the interaction between the people and their incumbent president or prime minister. Every reader, I am sure, harbours within himself a reasonably well organized set of perceptions and attitudes to these figures, but if each of us were to be asked singly how we arrived at our own particular constellation of reactions, I suggest that many of us would be hard-pressed to form any coherent answer, although each of us has been heavily stimulated by manifold emanations from both the exposed as well as from the more private essence of these public personages. Our conditioning to the outer world of experience, our reactions to the facts of these people as the world knows them, are surely significant in our ultimate personal evaluations.

Over the past months or years, we have watched our leaders with an eagle eye, mindful of their ideologies, scrutinizing them for their weaknesses as well as their strengths, cognizant of their talents and achievements, perceptive of their public deportment, and ever alert to each nuance, foible, and idiosyncrasy. We listen to their oratory and read between the lines; we observe their public image and look to catch every hint of a hardness or a softness, of a truculence or a tension; their excursions to Red China we follow meticulously and critically, burrowing and foraging for the morsels of gossip or political intrigue that might help us penetrate the 'private' domain of their personal lives. Anything that we or anyone else can discover about our leaders becomes more 'grist' for our own 'mills'. Every happening and experience through which these figures become involved in our outer world helps embellish, not only the concept we develop of their personalities and characters, but our emotional attitudes to their political policies as well. The experiential reality of our leader affects us profoundly one way or another.

But all these various stimuli alone hardly explain our *total* responses or the ultimate quality of our individual attitudes. The psychic soil on which the perceived public and private performance of such leaders implants itself is composed of ingredients that are varied and idiosyncratic in accord with the personal life experiences and situations of each individual in any given community. Citizen A, a farmer, is concerned about his crop and the market value of his produce; citizen B, his neighbour, is also alarmed by the erosion of traditional symbols from his culture; citizen C is a schoolteacher in an industrial city, with a deep aversion to anyone who reminds her of power or patriarch (her father beat her unmercifully as a child); citizen D, another schoolteacher, lives in a coastal town and has an aversion to intellectuals and sophisticates because her 'swinging' father abandoned her and her mother when she was a child; citizen E is an oil tycoon, against anything that threatens to disengage him of his money; citizen F is a hippy, against anything that threatens to take away his freedom. Outside the fact that each of these citizens is human, albeit living in different groups, in perhaps different nations or on different continents, what else do they have in common? On first look, very little. But this study will try to demonstrate that such separate entities, each with a group psychology as a framework for living through each also with individualized imprints from a variety of personal experiences, have none the less interwoven into the fabric of their beings a common skein of psychological process that identifies each with his fellow — a skein which, though issued in individual *colours*, when unravelled is exposed as being of the same creative *fabric* as that of his neighbour.

From all the interwoven threads composing man's common skein of psychological development, one in particular stands out as most significant to my thesis — *the mechanism of projection*, a psychic process in which the individual perceives his own psychological machinations as originating from outside himself. In discussions to follow, I explore the evolution of this phenomenon from its original matrix, the fusion that exists between mother and infant in the earliest days of a child's existence. Here I would emphasize only the timelessness and universality of this mechanism which is instrumental in the development of mankind's sense of reality. But psychological development may be arrested in any individual, and the mechanism of projection, instead of becoming a less important part of our psychic processes, may grow untrammelled and excessive, thus producing weaknesses in the reality-testing capacities of a society. I refer to a certain cluster of psychic and cultural phenomena (a social syndrome, if you prefer) that includes bigotry and xenophobia — and charisma.

Just as the infant or the young child demonstrates a strong tendency toward the use of projection in ascribing to persons outside himself those impulses, ideas, and feelings that are in fact of his own making, and just as primitive tribes continue to express in their cultures those same projective tactics, so, even in some of our more modern societies, do the needs of adult people demand some institutionalized and legitimized extension of this projective mechanism. Such needs relate to our efforts at unburdening ourselves of certain feelings of guilt that develop after we first become aware of the difference between our own strivings and those located in the outside world. The white man in North America, for example, is only now grudgingly coming to terms with a time-worn scapegoat, the North American Indian.

Projection is a significant mental mechanism that operates in all of us toward the construction of our basic sense of self. It is of interest that some psychologists (e.g., Klein 1932) have become so impressed with the durability and tenacity of projection as it operates in children that they have come to refer to *the projective position* as a definitive developmental phase in all child development. Anna Freud (1946) emphasizes that we quickly learn — on incorporating certain external authoritative figures to whose criticism we are exposed — to deny and ostensibly rid ourselves of those impulses that are vulnerable to such criticism ('project' means to throw forward, away from ourselves). We prefer to be initially critical of others rather than of ourselves. In effect, though we have learned what it is that is blameworthy, we prefer to negate who it is that should suffer the guilt. It is my contention that we use this same process of projection to justify to ourselves those ideals and objects of idealization whose worth we have learned otherwise to doubt and question. I have observed a number of people among my patients who have projected their idealized imagery onto certain political leaders (heroes). This matches Kohut's most recent observation on such projective phenomena (1971), where his patients' idealized imagery was thrown out and onto the figure of their psychotherapist (hero); Kohut describes these projections as necessary maturational steps in the psychological development of these patients.

Projection, then, is considered by many psychologists as a way of psychic life not only for primitive peoples and for children at one phase of their development but for many adults as well. In early times, man projected his fears and anticipations of doom onto such elemental forces as volcanoes, floods, hurricanes, and earthquakes; and well he might, considering that such natural phenomena, in our day, are apparently but faint reminiscences of the more violent elemental upheavals of an earlier time (Velikovsky 1955). As our technological advances have led to newer terror-provoking agents such as rockets, nuclear missiles, and so forth, all these new 'facts of life' are incorporated into the projective process. Though the process remains basically unchanged from one era to another, its psychological content naturally alters in keeping with the times. The anticipation of natural catastrophes served the persecutory needs of yesteryear's humanity just as, for example, the delusions of poisoning by radiation serve the paranoid of today (though this is a rather frightening illustration of the fine line between the subjectivity of projection and the objectivity of reality testing). Death rays, though still fictional, have already taken their place as weapons of self-persecution among the paranoid.

Everyone is familiar with the projective world of the child and how he disavows his own aggressiveness and omnipotence by foisting these tendencies onto his parents and friends as a justification for unharnessing his instinctual demands. If this process runs in high gear, the child is liable to project idealizations as well: the athlete he knows nothing about in reality is soon his hero. Augmented by the infective word-of-mouth of playmates, the youngster creates 'superstars' with an ease matched only by the ease with which he trades them in for newer and better 'superstars'. In many adults, of course, the identical process is visible: some are prone to offering projections as gratituitous information whether on North American Indians, on Jews, on the Blacks, the Chinese, or the Russians without ever having encountered any of these peoples in the flesh. It may be that nothing specific concerning such 'foreigners' was ever taught us, but rather that our early environment in some way encouraged and reinforced the projective tendencies of our childhood. I suggest that, to a degree, it is this self-same projection, this psychic 'hang-over' from our childhood, that often plays a part in also promoting those idealizations that give configuration to our charismatic objects of later years.

Just as the changing cultural climate determines the quality and texture of an individual's projections of disenchantments onto people and things that he considers bad, so do the cycles of culture mould the charismatic process of many people searching for newer and better vehicles to carry their imagery of the ideal. The creative process of charismatic imaging is as timeless as projection; it is something that has been intuitively known to mankind long before radio or television, projected as it always has been onto certain public figures through the available media in any historical period —

whether through the rabble gathered in the village square or through individualized communications by quill and courier. The political charismatic leaders of a Weberian era seemed as intuitive in their application of this group psychology as they were unwitting of its dynamics. Even in his pre-Fascist years as the young rebel secretary of the Forli Socialist Federation, Benito Mussolini had stumbled on the oratorical art of engaging audiences in the kind of unrehearsed political litany which is such a typical part of the group responses that help give birth to a new charismatic leader; even then, Il Duce was employing his own infectiously applauding claque to reinforce the mass projections of a gullible following (Hibbert 1962). For the political leader of today, television offers a more sophisticated instrument for promoting the identical process; the speed of today's imagery is faster than in Weber's day, its application of canned applause an even more infectious claque than Mussolini's. Television is today as much a receptacle for the projection of a people's imagery as the moon used to be; it is seen as an instrument for the incitement of violence just as the moon, a celestial and 'lunatic' scapegoat, was formerly believed to cause mankind's mental aberrations.

The media of today, as messengers of charisma, are but more refined versions of the more plodding vehicles of the past, all of them servicing the people and providing products, just like supermarkets; the product in the charisma business is the psychic imagery of the masses. Regardless of whether one refers back to another era where the creative 'word' was passed on in whispered message, or whether one relates the charismatic leader to today's more personified figurehead whose image emanates from an electronic device, there is a case to be made for the people as king-makers *par excellence*, as culpable agents in the elevation to charismatic stature of the one who fits the cyclical mood of the times.

The general outline offered here of charismatic imagery will, of necessity, suffer from 'de-realization', from an abstractness in psychic boundaries. The concept of a charismatic leader carving out his own public image purely from ingredients in his own personality is a singular and sharply defined configuration; by contrast, my concept of the charismatic image – one created by a mass of people evolving a process from within themselves, thence projecting it outwards onto a suitable chosen object – perforce must be a more de-realized and diffuse configuration, yet one significantly legitimized by the numbers of its reinforcing and worshipful participants.

I am aware that a psychoanalyst is but an 'armchair general' at best, an observer rather than an activist, and armed only with the limited implements of his trade. In many ways I could liken my vocation to the hobby of building model aeroplanes that do everything but fly. Though it is my aim to focus on those universal ingredients of our psychological nature that go into the creation of a charisma, I realize that this is only theory: such a model cannot comprehensively capture the truth of the phenomenon in general or in any particular. I am still open to Weber's idea that there may very well be some inexplicable x factor in certain individuals that enables them, unlike others, to activate and translate their drives to a fulfilment within the scope of the society around them. Perhaps only one who possesses this activating capacity is in a position to explain it properly, though I am sure that such a man or woman could hardly assist someone else in developing a charisma of his own. Apart from the possibility of its being genetically inherited, such a factor, if indeed it exists, would have to be categorized as unique and nontransferable.

Be that as it may, the argument I have chosen for trying to explain the charismatic phenomenon is one based on the personality dynamisms of all those citizens who, though seemingly passive spectators in the passion play of politics, are to a crucial degree the true instigators or inventors of that image of idealized man that I refer to as charisma, an image that is carried about within the psyches of all people in one form or another.

Chapter 2

The ingredients of charisma

The quest for an identity is the pivot around which this study of charisma revolves. The words 'identity' and 'self' are used interchangeably here, both designating the totality of one's mental images which are not only largely of a conscious nature but which have to do with one's social interaction with others. The self should be distinguished from the mechanics of the mind, which embody those three abstract agencies that constitute the psychic apparatus, namely one's ego, one's conscience (super-ego or ego ideal), and one's instinctual drives (id, i.e., aggression and libido). This chapter sketches the main diagnostic characteristics of the charismatic imagery in the self; a probing of how these features derive from the developing agencies of the psychic apparatus (ego, conscience, instinct) follows in later chapters.

To most modern-day psychologists, there is now only a slight disparity between those philosophies espousing a genetic or organic factor as a key element that gives root to one's earliest sense of self, and those doctrines which entertain a more developmentally oriented view of identity. Freud made reference to an individual's archaic heritage and his constitutionality. Existentialists have spoken of a primary self that crystallizes early in an individual's life, a self that carries from the very beginning all the strength and defined boundaries of an individuated organism; they have referred to this core as the 'I Am'. Similarly, the protagonists of religions and those belonging to racial sects have emphasized the spiritual and organic divinity of the individual from his very birth. Few rational psychologists dispute the importance of the natural psychological passions that revolve around the theme of one's organicity, and any therapist in the field of the psyche whose fundamental aim is to disturb or to dislodge such passions from their original genetic source is both unsound in his judgment and unwise in his thinking.

Yet it would equally be folly if one were to accept one's racial organic roots as the only fibre of one's mature and adult sense of identity. Such a view is a naive simplification, one that ignores that more complex and highly organized institution of the psyche called the ego. Clinically, the ego takes years in its development to achieve a state that can be rightfully labelled mature, and it is a premise of this study that only in the adult maturing years could any human properly claim a relatively well defined sense of ego. This by no means refutes the existence of a divine self or the absence of an existentialist's 'I Am'. Certainly the findings of psychoanalysis, both theoretical and clinical, make reference to one's ego ideal, a psychological abstraction that many theologians and sociologists prefer to call the 'soul'. Still, clinicians have little hesitation in suggesting that an early boundary-sharp sense of self is a rarity not only in children but in many adults as well. Nor is it possible to find in the infant or child confirmation of a particularly robust ego fibre; the ego is always infiltrated, well into adolescence and even into adulthood, by elaborate defences against the profound sense of fragility and helplessness felt by so many humans.

Rather, it is this multitude of omnipotent defences and exaggerated idealizations that form the early core of one's rudimentary conscience. And, from the standpoint of this study, it is this persistent core of heroic imagery, linked together with the more heroic elements of the conscience of the community at large, that becomes the mainspring of that image of idealized man which is charisma. Though one can accept as immutable the organic core of a being, along with the deeper passions intertwined with this core, it in no way follows that such root and its passions ordinarily remain immune to the screening and the filtering of an ever-growing ego; only this later development gives maturation to an individual's ultimate sense of relationship to the world and to the people with whom he lives. It is the ego that allows a pluralistic ideology for living, a necessary adaptation of people who wish to live side by side with others who differ in their organic and genetic heritage.

There are still many who reject pluralistic sentiment, convinced as they are that the homogeneity represented by a sense of racial and organic kinship affords the real cohesive force in the structure of any nation. The fact that such organic forces act subconsciously and are therefore not always amenable to the reasoning of the conscious will has been offered as a justification for their perpetuance. Naturally, those harbouring such an organicist ideology continue to perceive a pluralist society with doubt and suspicion; their logic still supports a segregation based on race and nationality as the natural law of humanity, a law they respect exactly for its organic validity. The polyglot humanity of the Americas, wherein millions of immigrants have common psychic ground with their neighbour, is perceived by such organicists as both the cause and the effect of a precocious idealism that has run away with itself. Even some of the less organically oriented political philosophers, such as Niebuhr and Sigmund (1969), warn that democracy too is a highly contrived form of communal living, basically dependent for survival upon organic foundations which, if given secondary status, could lead to total chaos.

People adhering to absolutist ideologies cannot be dismissed as crackpots. From their standpoint they are practical realists, convinced that it courts disaster to overlook the natural chemistry of a human being and to underestimate the power of the motivating factors derived from his national and racial origins in dictating his social behaviour and in deciding what he stands for in the world. They feel there is much to justify their views; they are well aware that 'birds of a feather flock together' and they apply analogies from the animal kingdom to human behaviour in such matters as herding, mating, and the struggle for survival. The question, of course, must arise as to whether or not one is prepared to view *homo sapiens* as following the path of the animal to the letter. Immediately one can find certain obvious paradoxes when it comes to human social and sexual behaviour, apparent contradictions to the natural organic laws. Though it may be largely true that humans do seek out other people of their own kind to love and to work beside, yet the history of human passions makes it apparent that an opposite holds true as well: the human appears to have a need to explore the unknown and even to seek out the stranger by whom to be influenced. Furthermore, he wants to influence that stranger — to mould him, to proselytize him, and even to love him. I cannot deal with the organic factors involved in this mutative phenomenon and so leave it to those in the field of genetics and transculturalism to elaborate on the biological implications. It is, however, a psychological fact that natural laws are compromised in many instances by certain human intrapsychic processes that seemingly operate in reverse. Clearly, certain psychological and philosophic elements creep into the whole picture at a higher level — an ego level — and these can and should be dealt with here in so far as they are related to the phenomenon of charisma.

One can think of several causes for such intrapsychic processes: a protest, a striving for independent behaviour that casts off the shackles of traditional proprieties; a more concealed effort that one could call counterphobic — a neurotic attempt to escape a human mating that might in any way represent something incestuous; or man's natural inclination to shake off the sameness and the boredom of inbreeding in search of new exhilaration. A later examination of this search for 'the stranger' may offer a more primary reason for both the fear of and the allure of the foreigner among us — something that relates to the child's ambivalent dependency during its early phase of separation from the mother.

THE CHARISMA OF THE FOREIGNER

The first characteristic of charismatic imaging is that the image contains the element of foreignness. The proverb, 'familiarity breeds contempt,' has a corollary: something foreign (yet familiar) breeds charisma.

One might wonder how accurate the popular opinion is that familiarity promotes disenchantment. Is it a matter of degree? True enough, one can say in general that, the greater the exposure one has to the more intimate elements of another human being, the more evidence one can accumulate to justify the contempt that one human seems capable of harbouring for the foibles of another. Yet there are certain degrees of familiarity with others which breed a form of narcissistic empathy, a kind of self-love, if you prefer. One can find sanctuary in this narcissism and refuge from the fears and associated hatreds that not uncommonly emanate from the unfamiliar and the strange. For all will recognize that too much foreignness can offset all the glamour of the stranger and that an imagery of danger begins to operate once one is beyond a certain threshold of comfortable estrangement.

The guardedness of nations in their international relations, such as exists between the western democracies and the Iron Curtain countries, is not only a reflection of their ideological differences, but their mutuality of fear of the stranger as well. The protective stance assumed by people for the safety of their leader when he goes visiting abroad among strangers, is reminiscent of the taboo of the early primitive cultures that Frazer described (1890): such a taboo on chiefs was specifically aimed at protecting a leader from the perils of magic and witchcraft emanating from any stranger. I suggest that the xenophobia among the great powers is very much of the same order. Among the preventative measures adopted in primitive cultures for purifying or neutralizing the danger lurking in the stranger, was the exchanging of gifts — 'common god' merchandise, as Frazer puts it. One can see this process of reciprocation in operation today between heads of state at a summit meeting or between Hockey Team Canada and their Soviet counterparts in their exchange of wood-carvings before playing their matches.

From the standpoint of this thesis, a more disarming technique is to convert a foreignness into something charismatic by the introduction of a touch of the familiar. It attentuates the danger and, providing the desired element of foreignness is preserved, it allows for the charisma that Nikita Khrushchev, for example, earned with the West when he broke the tension of the North American population: shoe in hand, he publicly pounded a United Nations Assembly table in a charmingly familiar gesture of childlike irascibility.

An intensification of familiarity then can cut below rejection and contempt and capture the narcissistic empathy that translates familiarity into delighted self-recognition. But the developmental processes of growth towards independence and away from 'family' cause, in many instances, the extension and displacement of our idealizations onto non-familial and less known figures of one kind or another. This is a half-way rebellious sort of emancipation, and there are many people who become fixed at this half-way level of individuation where only the less familiar outside figure becomes the acceptable object for admiration. A mature individual would respect both his own kind and the foreigner on their merits or capacities of personality, independently of kinship. To reach this stage one must reasonably pass through the infantile stage or idealization and the adolescent stage of disenchantment, overcoming one's earliest familiar attachments to parents and abandoning the quest for an adopted hero. At reasonable maturity, one would have an intellectual awareness of the degree to which one's biases in adult life for and against other people have been promoted by those emotions stemming from one's earlier relationships with parents.

Being an adult includes therefore a willingness to outgrow in the first instance our natural worship of only that which is familiar; such a homage is developed in our earliest years where the parent — even the most unworthy — is given attributes in the child's mind that represent the most acceptable characteristics of his psychic idealizations at that time. Second, being an adult must also include a capacity to outgrow our later predilections for aggrandizing and exoticizing the foreigner, whom we insist on endowing with all the most desirable virtues of the independence-seeking idealizations of our adolescence. Where before, virtuous attributes were reserved only for our own kind, at this particular secondary stage, our own kind now become recipients of our ambivalent derogation and disenchantment.

I suggest that the state of fully aware maturity is not all that easily or frequently achieved. The attitudes of any cross-section of humanity show this; even the most sophisticated people reflect those transitional reactionary dynamisms wherein the foreign or foreigner is given top status and the familiar bottom status in our personal values. All too often, it seems that the credentials for being accepted and recognized as an expert in our western society commonly include, among other qualifications, the status of a stranger. One's chances for promotion at work seem to increase with the degree of one's difference or dissociation from a home-bred image: 'the chief' will favour outside blood and bring in an 'expert' from Liechtenstein or a visiting professor from Bangkok; a physician or lawyer returning from studies abroad is received with open arms in his home town as an instant expert. Problems of competition and intramural envy may well be involved in these evaluations, but additionally there is a stereotyped presumption that the foreign expert is more competent than the home-grown and home-educated talent. An astute entrepreneur manipulates this human frailty consistently in the promotion of entertainers: 'Direct from a Special Engagement in Tibet' tends to bring box-office success.

Another generally accepted manifestation of the psychologically immature in our culture is the foisting upon us by certain individuals and groups of a pseudo-liberalism that pretentiously aims at giving the image of an enlightened community and so has to disguise the underlying and unsurmounted bigotries of their earlier development. Such liberalisms take on a typical fad-like quality; one year the Jews are 'in'; another year the Blacks; very shortly perhaps we'll have the Decade of the Yellows. This state of affairs may be progressive for a society at large, but I think it important to differentiate between this half-way affected posture and a more genuine progress demonstrated through the outgrowing by the ego of both polarities of infantile narcissism, the bigotry of familiarity as well as the idolatry of 'foreignness for its own sake'.

At the first stage of human development, then, one's family is the only acceptable thing and the foreigner is despised; at the half-way stage, a distorted enthusiasm for the stranger arises, often along with a contempt for the familiar. Often we rationalize this characteristic as being our own greater discriminatory maturity at work or our courageous capacity to rise above prejudice. But it is an immature and reactionary characteristic, which is often translated in terms of our attitudes towards a leader's ethnicity or towards his religious adherence or towards his national identity. This dynamism, above and beyond all political and ideological issues, played a significant part, I suggest, in allowing a German student activist to lay claim to an instant charisma on the campuses of France. It allowed a Canadian prime minister of both French and Scottish extraction, skilled, competent, and first-class as he obviously is, to hold that extra glamour in the minds of an Anglo-Saxon community. It helps explain the questionable heroics of an eccentric Britisher who became the saviour of Arabs, the captivating charm of a Jewish Disraeli rising to the heights in British statesmanship, an Italian Buonaparte leading the destinies of the French nation, an Austrian führer in a German Reich, and a Catholic American president in a Protestant majority. These, along with certain biblical figures, are but a few of the examples of this particular charismatic characteristic.

One might well speculate on whether Freud was unconsciously preoccupied with this theme of the foreigner in one of his later, more speculative, and controversial works, *Moses and Monotheism* (1939), in which he attempted to reappraise the Bible. He proposed that the Moses of the Old Testament was in fact an Egyptian rather than a Jew, basing his theory on a complex analysis of the psychopolitical and religious issues of the times. One must wonder whether in his twilight years, in the agony and pain of a terminal illness, Freud did not, on the one hand, recognize all the more urgently the ingredients of charismatic creativity in the Bible and, on the other, succumb to replacing biblical charisma with his own

personal romantic imaging. Freud might well have been showing in this effort some revived need to render as foreign that
which was for him most familiar (an example of one of
Freud's few indulgences in image-making; under the circumstances it is forgivable).

Men of science and of many denomi-
nations have chided Freud's creation of an Egyptian Moses as
an expression of an antipathy to things Semitic; writers such
as Roazen (1968) have diagnosed Freud's Achilles' heel as his
messianic elitism, a chronic hunger for a gentility expressed
through his robbing the Hebrew people of their spiritual
leader. Roazen's view is to my mind parochially narrow in
ignoring the 'family romance' complex on which I will elaborate in the next chapter in my description of the developmental stages of one's conscience. This complex lives on in
everyone to his dying day, being most likely to become exaggerated in one's twilight years as in one's formative ones.
Freud's Egyptian Moses is a study in the family romance of
the Bible, in the legend of heroes, and Freud in my opinion
was unwittingly 'hoist with his own petard' in replacing one
romance, the Bible's, by another — his own. Freud's speculations on Moses fit in well with his life-long atheism and with
the independence of his personality; he was a man who re-
jected all deities in his emancipation from a saviour and his
struggle to attain a supreme independence of spirit. By
'foreignizing' the biblical Moses, who in Freud's psyche
probably represented a familiar Jewish patriarch, was Freud
not in fact creating a charismatic object for himself?

THE CHARISMA OF IMPERFECTION

A leader with charisma is of necessity perceived as someone,
not only to a degree foreign, but to a degree *subtly* defective.
The victim of a massive bowel disorder or a rapidly progress-
ing malignant growth could hardly lay claim to a people's
charisma any more than a leader undergoing a major nervous
breakdown; the group response to such unsubtle misfortune
would be one of mingled pity and horror. But a candidate
blessed with some more minor blemish or stigma (such as a

slight limp of questionable origin) carries an extra dimension in vital imagery, one capable of capturing a people's imagination. Eisenhower's popularity with the people was significantly enhanced when, in his presidential campaign against Adlai Stevenson, he suffered a mild stroke; his popularity soared — according to a Gallup poll, from 61 to 66 per cent of the forthcoming vote.

In the realm of psychic quirks, a leader prone to an intriguing fear of wild geese or an allergy to green cashmere sweaters has a headstart for instant glamour on the leader plagued with a flagrant psychosis. Looking at Moses again, we note that in the Old Testament he was a stammering Moses, a man with a speech defect of unknown cause and yet capable of incisive and profound oratory. Here again is a 'straddling' characteristic (as in the foreign but familiar), giving a leader the best of two worlds. Here we have a stigmatized personality, but with just a slight stigma — just enough, perhaps, to have helped sway Freud, in his narcissistically creative terminal state, to adopt the foreign theme of a Moses. Freud viewed the process of idealization as the quest for perfection, a striving which we feel we cannot achieve within ourselves and which we try to effect in a round-about way by idealizing an outside object. My thesis suggests rather that the image of an external charismatic figure is embraced because of its slight imperfection; it is something attainable by all of us and therefore a narcissistic image that supports our convictions of our own charisma by its confirmation in the outside object (originally the mother).

Subtly stigmatized charismatic figures abound in biblical texts, and scholars in mythology such as Robert Graves (1948) have made efforts to link the theme of 'kingly' physical deficiencies with ancient ritual laming ceremonies (wrestling matches) that were part of the ancient 'coronation of kings'. As examples, Graves cites the lameness of Jacob in the Old Testament (Genesis XXXII) and that of Jesus of the Hebrew Talmud *Babli Sanhedrin* and the *Tol' Doth Yeshu*, as well as the 'bull-footed' Greek God Dionysus. Graves touches on the oedipal theme of castration in ascribing such lameness to the ritual symbolic emasculation of sacred kings as an archaically derived punishment for their sexual union with sacred queens (Oedipus was also deformed in the leg — which is what his name means). Graves puzzles with the enigmatic question as to whether such kings were chosen *because* they had accidentally suffered such an injury, or whether the injury was inflicted on these kings *after* they had been chosen for regal status. To my mind, in his preoccupation with the physical deficiencies of kings, Graves comes unwittingly close to the deeper theme of mother-child separation. In his story from Hosea xii, of a Jacob who in this version wrestles his twin Esau while both are still in their mother's womb, the symbolism depicting man wrestling with his twin (tripping up his own double) in my opinion captures the theme of one's infantile struggle with one's own narcissism (double) for an immortal union with the mother (in this example, in an intrauterine struggle). Interestingly enough, Graves favours the premise that, rather than supplanting Esau's birthright to a kingdom, Jacob won his sacred name and inheritance through 'the rights of maternal endowment' that existed in that historical period; he believes this factor was censored by the 'patriarchal editors' of Genesis.

Communal myth, an accurate reflection of the conscience of any given era, continues today as always to carry this theme of deficiency whenever the image of the charismatic hero is portrayed on stage or screen. The scriptwriters and impresarios of today's communal myths are flagrantly and yet unwittingly pushed to introduce this stigmatic theme. More often than not, their efforts to glamorize deficiency result in the elevation to pseudo-charismatic proportions of the most abysmal distortions of the human psyche. The sole claim to a charisma in such modern 'heroes' rests on their exposure of all the embarrassing personal deficiencies that most of us struggle to submerge within the deeper confines of our own unconscious. As with the jokers and clowns of the Shakespearean era — deformed creatures of one kind or another who sporadically appeared on the stage — some of today's television casts in leading roles freaks of one variety or another, strumming guitars to the accompaniment of tremolo, grimace, and rolling eyeballs. Such a 'sport' may offer viewers a satisfaction reminiscent of the Spanish bull-fights, with their false claim to elevate the humanity of both entertainer and spectator.

We may pay homage to the illusion that everything damaged in man is but the insufflation of a divine spirit at work and that a sacred deformity need not wait for its compensation in a world beyond. But, as always when people push their luck, exaggeration ultimately fails in creating a charisma; for 'two tablets are not better than one', and the glamour of the man with a limp is not increased if he has 'two heads'. Efforts at effecting a charismatic personality by introducing defectiveness fail unless the defect remains slight and empathetic.

There are also those sophisticated radio and television shows that produce more acceptable helpings of slightly damaged heroes for our entertainment: neurotically tainted members of the 'men in white' profession wander the corridors of our institutions of mercy; adventurous law enforcement officers, overweight and blinded, retain through a hypertrophied sense of sound or touch, the capacity to protect the people from the forces of evil. The message of these shows is loud and clear — a little extra fat and a wheelchair can be ingredients of charisma. It is not inconsequential that somewhat paralysed and battle-scarred figures such as Presidents Franklin D. Roosevelt and John F. Kennedy are among those who have found a place among the charmed circle of charismatic heroes, as have a lisping Churchill, a semi-dwarfed Buonaparte, an eye-patched Moshe Dayan, a lamed Byron, and an alcoholic Dylan Thomas.

Without a foreignness, then, that still manages to carry a flavour of familiarity and to symbolize one's roots, and without a subtlety of defect, a leader's potential for an image of charisma is seriously imperilled. All the straddling characteristics of the half-way stages of human emancipation from our infantile ties give us assurance that such a semi-independent leader is not as aloof and as remote as he would like us to believe; we sense, from our own imagery, that he needs us as we need him.

Pioneers of space may fly to planets, but if perchance they entertain any hope of a people's charismatic bouquet awaiting them on their return, they are in for a jolt! Their chances are on a par with those of the Martians, or of Peary who discovered the North Pole. The people of this planet have no charisma to offer anyone who discovers bleak and virgin places in space or on the Earth. We made Lindbergh a hero for 'shrinking the Earth': we were less than jubilant when the astronauts 'extended the cosmos'. Ensconced in his space-womb of technical wizardry the astronaut does not need us! Despite (or partly because of?) NASA's great efforts in public relations, the celebration of the moon landings was little more than a duty performed in the mass media. Discoveries that take mankind from primal mother earth and threaten all our dependencies and attachments might well occasion awe, a quiver of respect and admiration, a fear of the uncanny, a profound separation anxiety. But there is no charisma for the astronaut.

Neither is there any for other kinds of pioneer, Nobel prizes notwithstanding. Researchers for medical science, for example, are busy over cells and viruses. To the public their very names, far less their purpose or functioning, are totally strange and meaningless; they too are discoverers of bleak and unfamiliar things. The 'good old' family doctor with his bedside manner has a chance of being charismatic, but not the much more 'foreign' surgeon, with his ghoulish and antiseptic operating gown. We perceive ourselves turned into a case number or reduced to a spine, a gut, or a brain; rather than being in the hands of a healer, we see ourselves in the clutches of a de-humanized robot. These 'men in white' do not appear to need us as persons. Such is the common stance of many 'professionals' today with their image of total independence.

The same aura of self-sufficiency, of being far removed from familiar and earthy human connections, can attach also to certain political figures, some of whom conceivably remain baffled throughout their careers by their inability to earn a charisma from the electorate. I think of Adlai Stevenson. Like the astronaut, the scientist, and the surgeon, he demonstrated capacities which one might have expected to earn for him some charismatic acknowledgment. Yet his aloofness caused whatever underlying vulnerabilities and imperfections he had to become lost to the electors: missing in their experience was the touch of a stranger who could none the less be felt as familiar. The remote political figure does not remind us of that cosy attachment to a loved one; in no way does he help us conjure up the vaguest traces of primal dependency. Anybody who would lead us to unfamiliar ground (such as the future) and has not an underlying shred of familiarity is totally disqualified in the scheme of charisma.

Those who do lead us to a promised land must play a game of masquerade and seduction, disguised in a foreign armour of innovation and break-through, transporting us simultaneously forwards and backwards: forwards toward an ostensible autonomy, but really backwards on a glamorous voyage home to the familiar ground of the past, a ground that fills all the requirements of the old dependent defectiveness that stamps our immortal union with the mother. Such a pied piper will entice us and be rewarded with the mass donations from our common psyche to that charismatic shrine — the symbol of the psychic imperfection of mankind.

THE CALLING

An ingredient that makes its appearance with startling regularity in the historically documented profiles of public charismatic leaders is a professed sense of being called to public service by some spiritual or divine force. There have been countless dictators, heads of state, and activists who have responded to such a call; a few have tempered this quality in their sense of communion with a higher Being by settling for a more humble, albeit more heroic, 'rendezvous with destiny'.

It was not because of some personal religious fervour that Weber (1922) was prompted to elaborate his concept of prophetic leadership and to apply this religious dimension to the study of society at large: he properly recognized that there was no human culture without some spiritual current or supernatural order running through that culture. Yet in this recognition, he disregarded the essential psychology of the masses when he defined his charismatic prophet as a pure individualist whose claim for charisma rests on personal revelation. He proposed two categories of prophetic leadership, the exemplary mystagogue who sets a moral tone for people (Buddha, the Indian guru), and the ethical prophet, an instrument for proclaiming God's will (Muhammad, Zarathustra). Yet neither category satisfactorily explains the divine calling of a charismatic Communist such as Ho Chi Minh or the inspirational thrust of a saintly Hindu activist such as Mahatma Gandhi.

More relevant to this ingredient of calling are the writings of Emile Durkheim (1915) whose concept of a soul drew from the study of the Australian aborigines and their view of the human body as a shelter for the principle of life which animates it — the human soul. It is of some interest that certain tribes in such primitive cultures exclude the female as one that could harbour such a soul, a concept glaringly refutable by the manifestly idealistic activism of the Bernadette Devlins and the Jane Fondas of our times.

Durkheim recognized the soul as something generally known to mankind as a conscience — for Durkheim a sacred part of self that stands in contrast to the profanity of one's physical being. He was impressed with the inspirational force of man's conscience, which, if it was not in itself of divine substance, at least possessed a spark of divinity. The soul for Durkheim was by no means a concept based on human illusion, but an entity supported on the realistic foundations of all those moral ideas and lasting impressions of an ancestrally derived conscience that transcends the fleeting vulgarities of day-to-day mental stimulation.

Durkheim saw society as the instrument that 'forces a soul upon humanity', which, though harbouring this moral conscience, is none the less never quite equal to that same conscience. In all of us, he observed, there exists a particle of the divine, a portion of those great ideas which are the soul of the group; the individual's soul is only one dependent link in the collective soul. It is Durkheim's thesis that the personality of man is basically impersonal and group-oriented and hence more 'soulful' than it appears if man is viewed by the individualist who embraces the personal senses and passions that enslave one toward an exaggerated uniqueness. Likening Kant's concept of a will that is exercised by general rather than individual human reason to his own view of the soul, Durkheim concluded that what catalyses such a soul is that by which the individual is 'compounded' with other individuals; in effect a calling is vitalized from one's bondage to one's fellows (the group).

When translated into psychological terms, such a premise derives support from those psychoanalytic observations on the nature of human idealizations that give content to one's developing conscience. Out of infantile narcissism and the early separation from one's mother come the first rudiments of conscience and ultimately the capacity of the child to idealize both the self and other selves (development of ego ideal). This is, to my mind, identical to the inspirational force of Durkheim's soul. We feel called to live up to the new ideal that is felt to be both inside ourselves and outside in others (originally the mother and father). Later, we become called in relation to members of the larger group. As we go on striving to live up to ever newer ideals, the tensions resulting from the discrepancy between what we are and what we feel we ought to be often express themselves, even publicly as with many leaders, as a professed sense of being called. Existentialists offer a conception of man 'being taken above' by his fellows, and this idea would support this same thesis.

Narcissism, then, is the cradle of the soul, the sanctuary of one's calling, a necessary nursery for that divine spark whose nutriment toward tolerance and respect for the ideals of others can only come from those others in the group. Yet there have been historical figures with callings whose intolerance and destructiveness toward others nevertheless managed to inspire the souls of countless people, this despite the fact that such prophets did eventually suffer the repudiation of an enraged humanity; still other supernaturally endowed figures, such as Joan of Arc, have been physically destroyed by establishments as heretics. It would appear that the calling of charismatic leaders emerges from a paradox in the soul of humanity; passionate though many are in their condemnation of called fanatics, there are as many others who harbour an equal passion for the inspiration that is afforded by the messianic leader who can bolster those human ideals that look for a salvation from an earthy oblivion.

We are ever prepared, in effect, to project our own abstract transcendence onto some external rescue agent (as we did earlier on our parental figures) so that we may confirm in the more tangible imagery of that outside figure, the valid existence of our own tenuously established calling. It is the tangibility of the leader's calling, as confirmed by his organized following, that rescues the ideals of one's individual 'soul'.

THE FIGHTING STANCE OF CHARISMA

I have already made passing reference to the fourth of my ingredients for the charismatic image. I call it a posture of polarized aggression, a posture derived from the 'romance' of an individual's developing conscience. 'Romance' here is not to be confused with its popular meaning of love affair: rather it identifies a certain stage in the evolution of a child's idealizations (detailed in the next chapter) when in disillusionment, he turns from his parents in search of an extra-familial hero or heroine to adopt. This romance is intricately associated with the developing hostility and rivalry between a child and his parent, and I would notice here that out of the matrix of two universal complexes in man's psychological development, out of his oedipus complex and his family romance, there emerges one of two psychological prototypes, namely a 'winner' or a 'loser'. The envy and sexual rivalry with a parent draws the child's aggression into an oedipal (or negative oedipal) conflict and the resolution that results, to a significant degree, determines the ultimate stance (winner or loser) that the individual will assume vis-à-vis his competitors of later years.

It also determines his projected image of his ideal leader (as winner or loser). The tendency then to polarize one's aggressions, to take sides, to declare oneself victor or victim, winner or loser, must ultimately express itself at the level of a people's projections onto their leader; the latter must in turn then become invested with a polarized stance; and the stance that heroically disposed people want from a leader is of necessity *a stand for action.* In effect, people looking for a charismatic object for this projection are searching for someone ready to fight with another person or persons and ready to become victor or victim, winner or loser. The imagery demands that the potential leader be prepared to win something or lose something — and with action! It matters not for charisma what may be the ultimate fate awaiting such a figure; the key element is that he symbolize, in his image, someone who is taking an active stand, taking one side against another. His personality, in fact, may have all the markings of a heroic loser; and just because of this, he may fit the ideal image of followers who look to project the heroics of their own polarized stance of losers.

The vitality of this imagery of polarized action is derived, I suggest, not so much from erotic instinct (as the term 'romance' might suggest) as from the instinct of aggression that plays such a crucial part in the warlike fantasies of one's oedipal complex. Parricidal ideas may provide the content of this aggressive complex, yet it will be my ultimate contention that the aggression implicit in the image of polarized action is derived from even earlier pre-oedipal roots springing from old rivalries in the nursery, in which the child would fight his fellow for the favour of the primal mother. Any leader reduces his chances for a charisma if he backs off from the fight that rekindles this childhood ambition in his vicariously organized following.

According to this thesis, it is mandatory that the stand of the charismatic leader not be in opposition to a mere abstraction or thing, but against another human adversary (even if such an adversary has to be invented). To illustrate, can you conjure up a boxer englamoured by people for his sheer physical performance at shadow boxing? Who has more appeal — the track athlete who races against time or the one who defeats a competitor at the tape? Would Lawrence of Arabia have won a charisma for helping the Arabs win against pestilence and disease or against typhoons or floods? Try to visualize what degree of charisma John Kennedy might have achieved if his candidacy for president had not been contested. Without this element of active interpersonal struggle derived from our early childhood experience, charismatic image lacks an essential substance.

THE CHARISMA OF SOCIAL STATION

Another salient aspect of the charismatic image is again derived from the content of the family romance. Through the ages and still in a democratic society, the theme prevails of social station. The characteristic markings of such station have undergone only slight modification in our times. Up to the end of the eighteenth century, social status was determined by birth; only an aristocrat whose image was automatically associated with material wealth could provide the status required in charisma. The industrial revolution and an increasing emphasis on political power and the acquisition of wealth eventually led to class distinctions based on materialism and to status distinctions based on vocational prestige. In the twentieth century, subtle modifications have served to perpetuate the original significance of birth and money in the imagery of charismatic leadership. Our present culture allows for certain mutations: a poverty-ridden beginning may now enhance the potential of a leader for qualifying as charismatic; the odds are even firmer if, from impoverished beginnings, he has moved up to become 'filthy rich'. The more ordinary lower and middle classes — the 'just comfortable' — are burdened with a doomed imagery as far as charisma is concerned. There is just too much deadly caution and stability symbolized in such a state of survival-oriented economics.

Part of living up to one's social ambitions is to be accepted as belonging to one's class and conforming to one's status. A political figure of high office is as likely to associate himself with a bubble-gum commercial on television as a scientist is to appear on a panel alongside a vacuum-cleaner salesman. Occasional exceptions to this rule stand out as glaring examples of social indiscretion — or as dramatic testimonials to our maturing egalitarian society. American astronauts back from a 'moon walk' appearing on a 'spectacular' TV show along with 'show biz personalities' acclaimed for best sound effects in a full-length cartoon is a surprising conjunction which may reveal something of the 'new culture'. Yet, generally speaking, the need to retain a hierarchy in society remains clear, in commonwealths and republics as in monarchies. A family name can quickly take on all the magic of aristocracy even in the most democratic societies, and regardless of the real achievements or merits of individuals bearing that family name, the hereditary factor in itself is still sufficient to invest these individuals with the stamp of magic. Nations such as Canada and the United States, both sprung from monarchical states, have subtly continued to 'nurse' aristocratic imagery derived from their mother countries, images which have permeated their political and social structures because of the psychological needs of a people to relive and repeat the theme of a psychically emancipated aristocracy that originated in the family romance. North Americans have managed to invest their culture with the same hierarchical system from which they ostensibly wished to purge themselves. The 'commoner' at Hyannisport who casually refers to 'Ted's place' not only accepts and spreads the mystique of the Kennedy compound but may also be expressing his dearest wish for a close kinship with that household and its power. Name-dropping is a common manifestation of this need to trade on the glories of an adopted aristocracy.

That material wealth commonly accompanies the charismatic image may appear, at first thought, as an incongruity: how could 'filthy lucre' be linked with a bright and shining charisma? Manifestly, money represents a glaring affront to all things spiritual; it is one of the baser elements of human life; as power, it is coercive and dominating, and it has provoked envy and hatred from time immemorial; it is a prime force of evil. Even in rich and developed societies, people abounding with money are looked upon with suspicion in 'higher' circles. It is not easy to immortalize or moralize money, and the state provides a framework for disengaging it from its owner and preventing him from taking it with him into his grave. Money can be like excrement: it is something to be expended, lost, or taken away without the consent of the holder. In this regard, it is in direct opposition to the attributes of immortality.

Yet money can help its owner to the qualities of glistening charisma. It depends on how the owner is seen to use it. If it transcends the service of survival and is utilized as a means toward gaining love, for example, and hence no longer is perceived as serving personal individualistic functions, then money appears to qualify as a power to be incorporated into the charismatic imagery of the people. At the level of individual psychology, the theme of money plays a central role in one's personal myth. The family romance complex is invariably permeated with fantasies involving aristocratic adoptions, providing nobility of birth along with material wealth; in such instances, money seems to become automatically cleansed. For money to qualify as a symbol of charisma, its origins, its use, its bulk, and its ownership are all points of vital significance. Money gained by accident of birth not only divests the beneficiary of any responsibility for having acquired it (even through ancestral theft or embezzlement) but allows the inheritor to become idealized for the social station that comes with riches without toil. Having to work for one's living reduces one's potentialities for a charisma, as does spending wealth on such real-life problems as security or survival. Small or modest sums of money hold no charisma: vast sums are another matter, especially when related to a heritage of birth.

But the most appealing way in which money relates to the charismatic projections of mankind is through the rags-to-riches saga of the self-made man. There is universal enthralment at the personal heroics of the man who moves from beggar to king; but his regality rests, not only on an initial acquisition of wealth, but also, as in the general case, on what he does with it. Tales of people discovering a first penny lying in the street and then laboriously becoming millionaires do not 'turn us on' unless the new rich spend it magnificently. There is little glamour to a tight-wad — except to another tight-wad. The theme of charisma attaches itself to wealth only when it is employed in the service of rescue, in a 'sugar-daddy' operation that fulfils the wildest dreams of those eking out a living.

At the communal level, materialism qualifies for approbation the hard way. The dangers of evoking envy, hatred, and even murder force the wealthy to employ various techniques for neutralizing the reactions of repugnance that a public harbours towards them. In non-democratic societies, the problem may be simple: the chief or the dictator is simply a man of unquestioned power and as such entitled not only to his own wealth but a good portion of everyone else's as well; sultans, Arabian chiefs, and Indian princes are born to such a divine right to money. In democracies, although the carry-over of the aristocratic adoption theme still permeates the ideals of the people, money that goes with royal or semi-royal figures need undergo no further special charismatization; this is not so with the holdings of a 'commoner'. His money must become refined by the processes of repression, disguise, and denial, in much the same way as body smells are removed by deodorants.

Our culture prefers generally to talk not of money but of securities, just as it prefers to talk of powder rooms, not toilets. Our stock exchanges, vast marble 'outhouses in the sky', make no direct reference to money, only to 'bear' and 'bull'. If the market collapses and your life's savings go down the drain, your broker gently informs you that prices are 'easing' or 'soft', a classic understatement in curious contrast to the forthright declarations of the gambling world where a winner 'falls into a barrel of shit' and a loser 'craps out'.

The matter of money can be concluded by the suggestion that its liaison with charisma relates as well to the fact that the economy of a nation has always provided a significant vehicle for break-through ideologies involving a reshuffling of the national wealth. The charismatic leader may be given *carte blanche* to redistribute money and to mediate the nation's finances; he qualifies as an inspector of the bowels of the nation; he is acting as the group mother, with a mandate to induce people to relinquish their money to the government with the same docility expected of an obedient child and his 'potty job'.

THE CHARISMATIC SEXUAL MYSTIQUE

A certain mystique of sexuality is perhaps the most popular notion of what contributes to the special gloss of the charismatic image. Unlike the polarized aggression that becomes enmeshed in charisma, the libido involved in charisma is much more flavoured, I suggest, with the subtleties and straddlings that typify the blemished and foreign elements. A diffidence of expression, an unassuredness, an equivocation if you will – this is much more the stuff of charismatic sexuality than the air of confidence and cocksureness that one might logically expect. Where the aggressive component in charisma is one of forthright commitment to bold action, the sexuality of the charismatic image reflects, in contrast, an aura of uncertainty and self-doubt; the ego of the charismatic figures whispers a libidinous plea for a confirmation from an outside world. The image says, 'I'm really not all that sure of myself ... please, I need your help ... I'm as unproven as a virgin ... winner though I am, I'm just a shy guy when it comes to sex!' How can we hold in regard such a figure of fumbling stupidity, especially now that we've arrived at an era of a full sexual enlightenment?

Let's scrutinize this issue. In examining these alternatives, confidence and diffidence, as explanations of charismatic sexuality, I would argue that, although modern man seems bent on clearing up the mysteries of life, yet in the area of sexuality and its ramifications mankind continues, now as always, to go out of its way to compound rather than to clarify the riddle of human sexuality. If we take a look at some of the examples of history, we see that most of the prominent charismatic images that have appeared in past decades have in fact embodied as their most prominent feature of personal sexual adaptation a certain ingredient of enigma, of still probing the mysteries of this universal human dilemma. Is it not fair to appraise the public image of Adolf Hitler's private life with his Eva as not being of the same 'take charge' substance as his image in matters of state? More contemporary charismatic political figures, both living and dead, could also be said not to have demonstrated a statesmanlike message of 'all is under control' as far as their private sexuality is concerned: the images of Franklin Delano Roosevelt, the Kennedys, Martin Luther King, Pierre Trudeau have the same undercurrent of disturbed ambiguity in sexual adaptation as had Napoleon Buonaparte, Mark Antony, Cleopatra, Lawrence of Arabia, the Duke of Windsor. One might argue that some of these figures have offered images of bold adventurers in sex; yet I contend that their daring sensual undertakings do not disguise the underlying frailty of sexual resolution that was often reflected in their chaotic personal adjustments. An equivocating mystique works also, of course, with charismatic film stars whose controversial sex lives only enhance their aura of glamour; their riddle of sensuality serves to appease the voyeuristic appetite of their fans, searching for mystery.

As in the world of cinema, the world of politics offers its prominent figures a broad tolerance of their personal expressions of sex. Through its projections onto public personalities, humanity at large finds a legitimate vehicle for vicariously deriving a reassurance about its own problems of sexual development and its ambivalence in sensual strivings. As the lives of some of history's notorious wenchmasters such as Mussolini and Henry VIII illustrate, some leaders, despite an underlying shakiness of sexuality, have sensed themselves a proxy for expressing overtly all the thwarted instinctual cravings of their public and allowed themselves a life and an image of sensuality, some forms of which society would ordinarily consider as bordering on the obscene. Sexual adventures never seem to have the same lustre as when they are performed by a public personality; all the forbidden things of sex — philandering, illegitimate children, venereal disease, perversions, and so on — only go to enhance such a leader's charisma. Though these sequelae to sex may appear on the surface to reflect an experienced knowledge in matters of the flesh, they in fact only confirm a troubled and confused sexuality. A private nonentity, apprehended in sexual transgression, would be promptly indicted by a community, yet for the charismatic public figure there is a twinkle of delight, a quickening of the communal pulse, even a championing of his sexual capers, a support that becomes rationalized on the grounds that a leader's rights to privacy and to an equanimity of mind and body are all-important to the smooth running of the state.

In truth, the deeper cause of such approbation rests in large measure on the empathy that humanity harbours for the leader who dares to live out what his following only dreams. When we give our charismatic political figure our vote, we offer him a 'sexual allowance' as well. In a crisis, we want him relaxed; he can have an affair with an ostrich — so long as he is not 'uptight' in solving the crisis.

Despite popular tolerance and indeed enjoyment of a charismatic leader's uninhibited sexual activities, I still maintain that what people project to form the charismatic image is sexual diffidence. The leader is both a physical and a mental embodiment of an enigma. In the chapter to follow, the roots of the child's primal interest in sex and the origins of his preference for its mysteries will be traced. Suffice it to point out now, that man's universal curiosities and explorations with the earliest sexual activities of his parents is the setting that first inspires the mystique which the adult seeks desperately to recapture as a familiar yet mysterious complex lurking within the projected image of his 'adopted' charismatic object. This earliest matrix for sexual charisma, this 'primal scene' as it is referred to in psychological terms, is the original blueprint for man's sensuality, one that is first drafted by us as children as we imagine what goes on under the sheets of our parents' conjugal bed. From the earliest glimpses of parental nudity and from the earliest sounds of parental coitus, whether real or imagined, the child derives the mystique of his own sexual charismatic imagery. Herein lies the mainspring of man's need to perpetuate a confounding of all his reality-testing measures when it comes to his sexuality; his aim is to preserve the essence of libido as an endless enigma; the price he is willing to pay for this is the denial or repression of a full awareness in sexual matters. When it comes to his selecting a charismatic object in his adult life, he continues to draw upon this reservoir of sustained mystery that originated with his earliest responses to the primal scene.

Prominent then among the ingredients of charismatic imagery is a certain enigmatic tang extracted from the human penchant for preserving this vital element of mystery and illusion surrounding sexuality. The most popular riddle is 'who is doing (or not doing) what to whom under the sheets?' Our sex educators, even in primary schools, are diligently engaged in stripping away the mysteries from the minds of children with charts and diagrams of sperm colliding with eggs; yet they get slim rewards, for they believe, erroneously, that they are far more knowledgeable and adapted to the facts of life than those they teach. The popular psychology that finds repressed sexuality indicative of ignorance or of a deep maladaptation from childhood ignores the fact that in many instances the most diligent efforts to dissect, to analyse, or to lift these so-called repressive barriers against sexual knowledge only serve to reinforce equally tenacious efforts on the part of the human to submerge into lesser consciousness those sexual elements that afford the mystery his ego finds necessary to preserve. An analysis of their sexuality is for many as joyless as the analysis of their humour; if analysis of one's sexuality proves thorough or complete, then, as with humour, sexuality may well lose its spark and a grey barrenness be all that remains.

It is no mere coincidence then that in our 'espionage' approach to political figures, we demand colourfully diffident personalities 'on stage' to add their sensual spice to our charismatic needs. Every age produces its own sexually charismatic headlines — the Chappaquiddick tragedy, the Gerda Munsinger scandals, or the Profumo affair, or simply anecdotes that embellish the nocturnal readings of a people seeking to invade the private lives and boudoirs of intriguing public figures in high places. It is not surprising too that, no matter how desperately our swinging youth tries to reform the sexual mores of our society with expositions, nudities, and a 'show all' and 'tell all' liberality, the sexuality of charisma none the less continues. It defies this onslaught that would rob charisma of its very lifeline to mystery, a lifeline that through the ages has supplied this esoteric nutriment of psychological content. The mystique surrounding a sexuality that is hidden rather than exposed, that is unknown (illusory) rather than known — this is the substance of charismatic sexuality; here, everyone has the opportunity to be a 'private eye', everyone can engage in voyeuristic intrigue, snooping and ferreting for every shred of sexual innuendo attached (not coincidentally) to the chosen charismatic idol.

The wisely coached and properly trained political figure aspiring to a charismatic niche is well advised in the shrewd application of these insights into human foible. The way he presents his sexuality to the public — or rather the way he disguises it — is a vital aspect of his political equipment. If he comes on strong to the public like an amateur strip-teaser without her G-string, he is finished; some of his sexuality must at all costs remain private. The appeal of the strip-teaser rests not with her nudity but with her G-string. It is in the no man's land between what is exposed and what is hidden that the story of charismatic sexuality takes place. We deplore knowing too much of our idol's mind and personal chemistry; we demand our right to remain puzzled.

The thesis then to be derived from all this is that the sexual aspect of the charismatic image is mottled with all the perplexities and heavily cloaked immaculacies of a basically infantile sexuality rooted in one's curiosities that go back to the primal scene. It follows that the sexual imagery, both attributed to and often earned by the charismatic leader will relate itself especially to this aura of puzzlement. The leader who commands a forthright image of responsibility and mature adult adaptation in the area of sex must forfeit thereby his claim to any charismatic sexuality. Conversely, the leader who captures the essence of diffident sexuality, who manifests an aura of childlike perplexity to his sexual chemistry, whose private peccadilloes and sensual indiscretions show that in sexual matters he has, as it were, both feet firmly planted in thin air — such a leader has indeed taken a giant step toward charisma.

THE CHARISMA OF HOAX

Yet another salient characteristic of charisma is best described as the element of play, of make-believe, or hoax. It has been observed that every great politician is to some degree an actor. In this day and age of electronic communications, I believe that more than ever this impression is accurate; our political figures on the national and global stages are thespians of the first order. Such an opinion debases neither the profession nor the people who demand this quality in their leadership. By and large, people have always looked to their leader for colour, for someone capable of stirring them to emotion, either by some action, by posturing, or by the 'immortal' lines leaders seem inevitably compelled to deliver in one form or another.

Is it pure coincidence that we find in political leaders especially this wide range of histrionic abilities? If one adheres to the premise that we the people demand this sort of thing, that we the followers have something built into our psyches that cries out for a show from our leader — if one accepts this, then the question is to a large degree answered. I, for one, believe that the leader is very well aware — grudgingly in many cases — that what the people want among other things is an actor; and that is just what the people receive. Acting, as contrasted with action, certainly contains a significant element of hoax. The politician purposefully creates an illusion or an impression of himself that does not in fact fully coincide with the reality. He is engaging in a cold-blooded misrepresentation — and this with the blessing of his public. The leader, if he believes his people want a strong person, is capable of acting strong; when they want humility, he can act humble. This behaviour has to be labelled hoax.

Hoax is one of the least understood elements in human behaviour, but it has a place in the fabric of charisma. It would seem to follow that we who demand such acting, such theatricals, such elements of hoax from our political leaders, must be equally endowed with at least a sprinkling of hoax. Somewhere in our personalities and in our character structure there must lurk our own theatricals, our own excitement with deception, with illusion, with play, and with hoax. It is no mere perversity of human character that prompts a secret exquisite delight, which we often then try to stifle, when we hear of a fraud smoothly perpetrated by a hoaxter, especially when the victim is some large impersonal bank or industrial corporation or governmental institution. Often we feign a righteous indignation as a demonstration of our own personal integrity of character; but, underneath, how many of us do not cherish the naughtiness of the whole affair!

It follows further that the leader who is to capture our sense of familiarity and empathy with this element, the leader who can play our game and read our script with the proper intonation, is taking yet one further step toward clothing himself with the attributes of our charisma. And it is all-important that the leader who plays at hoax should play it well. The people require at all costs that their participation in this political charade remain disguised to a reasonable degree from their own awareness; by the same token we want our proxy, our leader, to conceal his participation as well. In substance, we want our leader, if he is to indulge in hoax, to be exceptionally good at it or not to indulge at all.

For the purposes of this discussion, I should like to confine the term hoaxter to a more normal personality whose characteristics can be found in varying shades in just about everyone. It has been said that there is not a human without a touch of larceny to him, and I would extend this generalization to include a touch of the hoaxter as well. Like the medical student who becomes 'afflicted' with all the various diseases he encounters in the clinic, so the student of human psychology soon comes to discover all the traits in himself that are qualitatively identical to those of his subjects of investigation. And one of the most unpalatable aspects discernible in oneself is that of the hoaxter. Everyone has at one time or another behaved as though he were endowed with capacities that he knows he does not truly possess. The wish to convince others and often oneself that one is more knowledgeable, more proficient, and more expert in something than one really is — this is the substance of hoax. Our ideals at times inflate us into adopting a posture of having already arrived at everything we wish to be.

What is the affinity of hoax to charisma? Both images are strongly connected with narcissism for one thing. Just as there is a certain narcissistic charm to the charismatic leader, so there is a charm to the hoaxter. Both carry the stamp of seemingly independent and autonomous people, and a certain festive aura is a most striking feature surrounding these two types of personality. The public is a 'sucker' for both. Given certain conditions, we find ourselves pulling for their success, for in both instances they offer us a release for our own unresolved hoax, a respite from our own strenuous efforts to prove that we are everything that we know in depth we are not. Just as we see ourselves in the charismatic figure, so we see ourselves in a hoaxter. We respond to the possibility that, through them, the long-haul achievements of traditional struggles will be proved unnecessary. The success of both such figures in our culture represents for us a victory for our jeopardized self-esteem, an uplift from the depression and helplessness that would infiltrate our awareness, expose our limitations, and force us into a recognition of all those failures that we find most difficult to reconcile. Through both the hoaxter and the charismatic leader, we can express our contempt and our derogation for traditional fathers, including the 'great man', a contempt that permits us to turn back the clock to play in the nursery, to make-believe, to pretence, and to mimicry; in this we hope to postpone or permanently avoid the anxiety that would come from the relinquishing of our hoax and the unmasking of our true ego. Both the charismatic leader and the hoaxter then provide us with a short-cut to an identity, a quick solution to the agonizing problems of maturation; a hoax obviates a commitment to any performance involving a steady drainage of our energy, for we have little hope of its continued replenishment, unlike the hoaxter living off a pipeline. The hoaxter has a life-style that rejuvenates him, 'charges his batteries', and keeps his illusion of perennial youth intact.

Like the charismatic leader, the hoaxter offers a combination of paradoxical ideals. On the one hand, he demonstrates a kind of reckless independence in which he thumbs his nose at the world; on the other hand, he displays a desperate unwillingness to move beyond an intense dependency on the same world he would deceive; he assumes a posture of both wanting nothing and wanting everything from the society in which he lives. As with the charismatic leader, the hoaxter attracts us and fascinates us with a charm that emanates from that most hypertrophied element of his personality, namely the element of play. This nursery aura gives him a magical make-believe essence that is peculiarly endorsed by an overlay of credibility and legitimacy. Even at the heights of our enchantment and homage to the charismatic leader, the discerning part of our psyche, though allowed a temporary freedom and suspension from judgment, still whispers to us that something make-believe is going on. To prevent the truth from breaking through, we search out all those affirmations from our environment that will support the illusion and neutralize the threat of any eruption from our more critical faculties; we want the play to continue, we want the show to go on. And so we derive reassurance from the crowd at political rallies, we take comfort from the media that reinforce our seduction; we help disguise those elements of pretence that threaten the play and we cast out the cynic who would disturb the glamorization.

Providing the charismatic leader plays our melody reasonably well, we struggle against any disenchantment of our own idealized theme. And if he plays it brilliantly, we can be wholly enchanted and seduced. In much the same way we treat the hoaxter; we protect him from becoming too blatantly a hoax; we insist on bestowing upon him some essence of charisma; we insist that if he is going to be *our* hoaxter, then he do the job professionally; we want a competent, slick performance: we will not tolerate the emergence of an underlying integrity or an overdone fraudulence, for either would spoil the whole show.

The play element in hoax is an element that begs our participation, our co-operation, and our protection from an infiltration by overly realistic forces that might disturb our 'suspension of disbelief'. The aura and atmosphere surrounding the play, the props, the co-operative audience — these are most significant features in any *group hoax*. The people in the stands at the professional football games are, if anything, more important for hoax than the players themselves. In the roar of the crowd lies the vital dimension of approval and participation, the protection of the illusion superimposed on the instinctual gratifications also served by the action. This mass confirmation gives a legitimacy to the players and the audience alike; it disguises any escapism or any elements of hoax associated with the entire happening. Appropriately enough, the activities of the neutral referee (who may be trying to win for himself by his skill in controlling the game) conveniently support the element of collusion in anarchy that often underlies such a group hoax, though there have been occasions in our time when berserk spectators have carried out their threats to kill the referee for his anarchistic interference in the 'play'.

THE CHARISMA OF INNOVATIVE LIFESTYLES

An appropriate last ingredient on the list of personality spices blended into charismatic imagery is that especially communicable facet of social deportment which we might call *innovative lifestyle*. The old axiom that a change is as good as a rest particularly applies here; one seeks respite from the staleness and the boredom that is a part of everyone's life at one time or another through finding some change in lifestyle. Our regular shifts in fashion for living reveal on a deeper level our hunger for recapturing the playful delights and fresh first experiences of our childhood years. In addition to the foreign elements tied in with our need to savour new, colourful, and exotic things, whether in food, clothing, social influence, or excursions to distant lands and new faces, there operates in us as well a striving to relive and repeat those first experiential delights of our infancy and childhood, where familiarity, as in charismatic foreignness, is both hidden and secured by the overlay of new modes for practical living. New fashions in clothes often take their inspiration from fashions of the past, thus providing an obvious real-life example of the blend of old and new, the known and unknown, for which mankind craves.

The ingredient of innovation that becomes embedded in our imaging of a charismatic lifestyle is illusory; the actual experience we seek may appear new, but the delight in experiencing it goes back to those early delights of our childhood, when we first savoured sweets, or slept at a neighbour's, or gave up fighting, and felt our first sexual awakenings. It follows, in this thesis, that the leader who, in his own public deportment, assists us in recapturing this familiar aura of a delight in change is well ahead in his claims for a charisma. He thereby captures the innovative lifestyle imagery of millions; it is not youth alone who look outwardly to project this innovative image, but older citizenry who continue to search for that someone outside to match and so to confirm the value of their own search for the delights of novelty that is deeply remembered from childhood. Even people in the twilight of their lives are ready to become infected all over again by the rejuvenating climate promoted by a leader whose image can support the dream that it is 'first time round for everyone'!

Each of the characteristics described in this chapter plays its own significant part in the over-all composite that is projected by the public: spice of foreignness, some subtle stigma, the calling to public service, a posture of romantic polarized action against a human adversary, an aura of social station and its associated wealth, a diffidence of sexuality, a coating of hoax, and an allure of lifestyle innovation. These are the eight elements of charisma. The presence of each and every one is not mandatory for the image: yet an absence of one or more of these ingredients can only serve to reduce the charm of a public figure in quest of a people's charisma. One atom missing from a molecule or one chemical missing from a compound can alter the power of the larger entity; so it is with charisma. A romantically polarized aggression toward a human adversary coupled with an enigmatic mystique of diffident sexuality — the two main ingredients — might yield, if unembellished by such essences as a foreignness or a subtle deficiency, not the true 'elixir charismaticus' but, alas, a robust precipitate of non-charismatic sludge.

Chapter 3

The fertile soil

The phrase 'the masses' has a different meaning for different people. To the elitist and the powerful among us, it may conjure up an image of a throng of low-grade blobs; to the grass-roots realist, 'the masses' may signify all honest humanity, basically oriented to earthy and concrete matters, devoid of the complexities that a more sophisticated person would imagine; to the more psychologically oriented, the masses are commonly perceived as people in one way or another swayed in their perceptions of their internal and external environment by intricate forces which are, to some significant degree, unconscious. It is this last definition that is used here.

The dynamisms that I ascribe to this large segment of any existing society are findings directly resulting from the well-documented efforts of psychologists such as Freud; and they include, as well, my own clinical observations. Behaviourists, taken as they are with their own versions of the human psyche, will label such clinical material as unfounded assumption or juvenile exercises in mythology. I rely, however, on the versions of those who believe that the evolution and the growth of one's sense of identity is a slow and tedious process; to a psychologist, each person must undergo agonizing confrontations with the problems of inhibitions, of fear, and of conflict in his thrust from an infantile position of primal dependency and fusional identity, in his struggle to pick his way through the magical world of his omnipotence, his idealizations and then of his disenchantments, making his ultimate way toward a reasonable independence and individuality.

The masses are made up of you and me, a collection of individuals each with his own intricate psychic apparatus. It seems only reasonable, if we are to talk about such an apparatus *en masse*, that we start first with an examination of the individual psyche and then determine to what degree and in what way one's psyche becomes modified as one blends into the group structure. One's individual sense of embryonic self is the 'gut' matrix of everything that grows toward the making of one's own charisma, one's own image of an ideal leader.

Freud regarded one's earliest identity as narcissistic — or primarily egocentric if you prefer: no other object than the self is taken into account in establishing the earliest sense of one's identity. In his original work on dreams (1895) Freud expressed the conviction that the aim and end of all thought processes was to bring about a state of identity rather than to consolidate some primary pre-existing sense of self. He felt that thought whose energy revolved around body image was primary in establishing one's earliest basic identity, and he conceived of the sense of reality as originating from the projection of sensory perceptions of one's own body in earliest infancy onto objects outside it, the external object (mother) thus being perceived by the infant as a part of the child that had been severed from its own body and thereby lost.

By contrast, other psychologists such as Balint (1960) have more recently ascribed all narcissism as secondary to the most primitive of human relationships, the harmonious interpenetrating mix-up of primary object love between mother and infant. Balint states that all the ensuring consequences in which the infant slowly separates itself from the mother involve varying degrees of the infant withdrawing love from its original object, the mother, back onto itself and that such withdrawal of love, a narcissism if you will, is purely secondary to the original primal love between mother and child. For our purposes of understanding one's earliest identity, both these views, Freud's and Balint's, though they may affect our later theorizing on the origins of a group psychology, none the less cause little alteration in our understanding of the development of earliest individual identity. Both theories in fact explain many psychological experiences in our childhood as well as in our adult lives.

INFANTILE SYMBIOSIS

I suggest that Freudian theory, backed up by the clinical perceptions of people such as Spitz (1950), Felix Deutsch (1959) and Mahler (1967), can allow one the conceivably sacrilegious assumption that one's dimly perceived view of oneself as a neonate involves a definite confusion of one's body with that of one's mother. In such a view, the infant's first awareness of itself after birth would be one of being severed from its mother, though the infant would not, of course, perceive the mother as such in this early phase. The mother for a time remains very much a part of one's self; some part of self is being severed from another part of self. Now, psychologically, the infant should not tolerate this state of affairs very easily; there would be a natural attempt on his part to restore the loss of his own body wholeness; that outside part of him that is eventually to become his mother would appear to remain for a long time united with his own body. How could this be accomplished? Psychologically speaking, the only way would be to incorporate the mother back into his body by symbolizing some aspect of the mother as an existing part of his own body. This seemingly bizarre hypothesis does in fact explain and clarify the clinical observation that, under certain conditions of the threatened loss of a loved person (such as through sickness or death), children and many adults do commonly experience symptoms in the parts of their bodies that have so become symbolized in their infancy.

To the infant then, the mother for some time logically appears as belonging to him, as a part of his own body; outside himself, she would appear severed as well, *damaged* if you will, as helpless in fact as the infant feels himself to be. Only together as one unit are the two, mother and infant, likely to appear, within the realm of the infant's early psyche, as whole and sound. This state of affairs can be labelled interdependency or, to use a convenient biological term, symbiosis.

Symbiosis cannot continue for as long in humans as it can in plant life. Sooner or later for sheer survival, there has to be some kind of a struggle for independence on the part of the child, some kind of effort to develop an individuality and a self-sustenance. Where initially, to all intents and purposes, he is just a vague symbiotically oriented bundle of instinctual forces, soon an institution in his psyche begins to develop, an abstraction which can be labelled the ego. This ego could be described as the executive branch of his developing self, an increasingly intricate adjusting and filtering mechanism for his perceptions and instinctual desires. This ego will ultimately develop a certain degree of organized independence, both from its own infantile instincts and from objects in the other world such as that mother from whom the child has such difficulty in separating.

As individuation proceeds, the infant must eventually begin to concede that the mother outside himself is not quite as damaged and as severed as she appeared to him earlier; as his individuality becomes realized, the damage of severance appears to become slighter. The mother would now be perceived by the child as only *subtly* damaged. Furthermore, as the infant acclimatizes himself to the concept of the mother being actually outside as a separate person, she would logically be no longer as familiar an object to the child as she formerly was when she appeared as totally a part of him at earliest infancy; the outside part of himself that is now, in his subjective reality, becoming his mother thereby becomes more *foreign* to him.

The whole process is by no means a smooth or unbroken evolution, but rather a to-and-fro struggle of separation, reunion, then separation again, the entire dynamism receiving its impetus from the independence-seeking energies of the infant's thrust towards a separate self. Gradual success in separation should logically lead to a lessening of the perceptions of familiarity towards the mother now crystallizing in the outer world and, as time moves on, the mother should become a more foreign figure and only a subtly damaged or defective object to the child's psyche.

The mother, albeit to a lesser degree than before, is still in need of being 'rescued' by the child, as is the child in (lesser) need of being rescued by the mother. By rescue I mean a psychological fusion between infant and mother, a merger that often subtly occurs even in adult people under stress. Such a fusion is elaborated later when I describe its reactivation in many citizens who need to cling at some deeper level to unconscious rescue images restimulated and re-evoked by a charismatic leader.

THE EMERGING CONSCIENCE

As the process of separation continues, the child begins to develop a conscience out of his ego. By conscience I mean more than a sense of guilt — rather, a distinct (abstract) institute of the psychic apparatus, which, in its most rudimentary form, is capable of helping the child form a value judgment of himself as well as of the mother now beginning to take more shape outside him; later this valuation process involves others as well. The development of this early conscience signals that the infant is withdrawing his love from the outside figure of the mother onto himself; at the same time the child begins to renounce his claims on the mother as a private love object for him alone. He does not simply abandon the mother, but avoids a profound sense of loss by the workings of a conscience that allows him to idealize and symbolize her continued presence in his psyche by a process of *incorporation*. He borrows some of her more significant attributes, by no means recognizing them as necessarily her better features; his ambivalence toward giving up his mother activates his instinctual aggressions toward the very object he now idealizes, as he symbolizes and incorporates aspects of the mother within himself; these are now felt inside him as damaged too. Here is an early example of a child hurting someone he loves. In effect, his idealized borrowings seem, paradoxically, damaged a little when taken back inside himself. (It is much the same with stolen money: we commonly think of the money rather than the thief as tainted.) It is the aggressive incorporation, then, of a part of the mother that gives the child the perception that something inside himself is damaged (Schiffer 1959). In adult life, the same ambivalent process, often associated with bodily symptoms, becomes reactivated in the psychological life of one who mourns the death of a loved one.

It is the damaged incorporated mother inside the child's psyche that causes him or her at such borrowing times to feel bodily pains; all children experience these to varying degrees and many people attribute these symptoms to sundry organic conditions; the child might learn from his grandmother that these are growing pains, or muscle spasms, maybe just plain nerves. It should be mentioned here that the tendency toward such symptoms, as well as the threshold of their intensity, appears to be an inherited or constitutional characteristic. Loss-burdened children (through death or divorce of parents) are naturally more prone to these bodily sensations, which have come to be known as 'conversion symptoms'; they are indicators of the paradoxical struggle for both dependency on and independence from the mother. There is both a taking in and a pushing out at one and the same time. Later on, such conversion signals might configure an elaborate network of symptoms in those bodily parts representing other key figures in the child's immediate life, such as one's father and siblings, who become psychologically symbolized and incorporated into the body scheme as well. I have reported (1959) on several cases of siblings, including a set of twin brothers, where one brother so idealized the bright mind of his twin that he developed the symptom of light-headedness that symbolized for him the presence of his twin's 'borrowed mind' lodged inside his own skull. As with a thief, who after his thievery, can neither use his own money let alone the money he has stolen, so it was with my patient's mental functions; in his light-headedness, he lamented his inability to use his mind for thinking things out. A loss of voice was the conversion symptom of yet another patient, who idealized and envied a brother whose profession as a clergyman required the cultivation of a gift for public speaking. In my patient's unconscious desire to borrow (incorporate) the powerful voice of his envied brother, he lost the use of his own.

Every psychiatrist encounters such patients in his private or hospital practice; and everyone experiences conversion symptoms in one degree or another, often without paying any attention to them. Adults as well as children, and of both sexes, undergo conversion phenomena. Young pubertal girls are especially prone toward reactivating their aggressive incorporation and symbolization of envied body parts of family members; such a process is commonly signalled by the abdominal conversion symptoms which are often confused with attacks of appendicitis. Commonly, the objects of idealized incorporation in such young girls includes a mother's or an older sister's bosom, or even a brother's or a father's genitals.

Father leaves his highly significant imprint on the child's psyche; though his relationship to the infant is different from that of the mother's, in that he gives neither birth nor breast, yet he too for the child becomes a passionate object for symbiosis, then for separation and ultimately for idealization, incorporation, and symbolization. Naturally the male genitalia, when coupled with the father's more aggressive role in the family, provoke that added quality of phallic power in the early idealized imagery of the child. Both boys and girls will aggressively incorporate and 'convert' this phallic power and only around the age of six will they both begin to settle for their own genital endowments, heightened for them in significance at this period.

To the observer of individual psychology, it is rather striking how much of a person's earliest sense of identity is achieved by symbolically incorporating others. The child could be described as basically a thief, if not in deed, certainly in the manner he mimics, emulates, and borrows from others. Yet paradoxically, through such thievery, come the first rudimentary contents of his individual conscience; his capacity to make a value judgment of himself first comes about by incorporating (stealing) some aspect of his parents. If, for example, he idealizes and incorporates a father who is among things a thief, a child may well be convinced that it is alright to steal. If on the other hand, his mother is merciless toward thieves, then the child may well develop a tendency both to pilfer endlessly as well as to chastise himself for such acts.

One rarely realizes the extent of these residues of infantile scavenging that still lurk in one even into adulthood, when they are often expressed as recurrent body symptoms. Many people display a veritable body language of such symptoms, a communication that often reflects an excessive preoccupation with matters pertaining to one's passion for an immortality, for a control over life and death (psychologically the perpetuated union with the father and mother). I have in mind a woman riddled with conversion symptoms in all extremities of her body (Schiffer 1962). These symptoms signalled this patient's control over her loved ones — family members who had either died or whom she was afraid would be lost to her in real or imaginary ways. A right arm, a left leg, or a ring finger, were chosen at different times to express her fear of loss or her fear of losing control over one or another member of her family. Her inherited predilection for utilizing conversion was aggravated by the premature deaths of close family members, and she struggled to make up for the loss through death of her mother by a compensatory incorporation of her husband and children.

Such thematic undercurrents are demonstrated in the inordinate interest that people show in philosophies having to do with a life after death. Automatically, it seems, we develop insurance programs in our quest for an immortality. The child finds himself playing the psychological game in which he creates doubles for himself, other imaginary selves, commonly endowed with features derived from both his parents. This is the stuff of which his growing pains are made. And he is largely oblivious of this process, oblivious to the possibility that in his creation of doubles and in other psychic measures to ensure longevity he is indulging in a rescue operation of both 'severed' parental figures. For they, together with his body, represent the minimum equipment necessary for his immortality.

To this point in the development of the child, the psychological foundations just described represent a fertile undersoil for the subsequent flowering of one's conscience. The psyche to this point, as at all future points of development right into adulthood, carries a potential for developing two alternate directions; either it can go forward toward maturation or it can go backward, especially if some threat comes along to make it necessary for the individual to reactivate the foreignness and damagedness of those early symbiotic years and seek its rescue by another person.

THE FAMILY ROMANCE

With each bump and knock, children beyond the toddling age begin to acknowledge some of the dangers of the world that is now taking more shape outside. All the more reason for them to redouble the insurance program they have already begun in their earlier years. Unwittingly they busy themselves further with their own portfolio for survival.

Not only do they try duplicating and reduplicating their possessions, whether sticks of gum, football cards, pencils, or crayons, but they learn how to manipulate the grown-ups around them in a tactic that gives their youthful personalities an aura of entitlement blended with a devious connivery. For a period, they may have all the makings of professional thieves as their passion for collecting things that belong to others begins to consume them. Their growing pains continue, especially toward nightfall when daddy robs the boy of his mother, and mother robs the girl of her father (oedipus complex); and the monsters and witches outside their windows threaten to rob mother and dad of their little 'jewels' (castration anxiety).

Daytime is more fun, with occasional shopping expeditions with mother, where they can lift a few goodies from the shelves in the grocery. In short, they are becoming kleptomaniacs. Later they will recall, with twinges of remorse, this particular compulsion to pilfer from the five and dime empire that was their childhood paradise. To their minds will come all too vividly that one occasion when they were apprehended by the store detective, and long after abandoning their life of overt crime, they will remain burdened with the guilt for those undercover capers. They will feel haunted at times with convictions of having stolen something without there having been a crime committed, never fully comprehending a guilt that stems from their unconscious preoccupation with robbing a parent of a wife or husband. Out of a stricken sense of conscience, they might make gestures at expiating for a crime that they never intend to repair, gestures yet sufficient to appease the kind of embryonic conscience that goes with their childhood compulsion to prove themselves superior to their own parent.

Fortunately for civilization, children do not remain either children or thieves. Their conscience begins to mature; with increasing demands for independence, coupled with a growing sense of self-respect, their whole character gets a forward thrust toward the renunciation of those aggressive needs that would stake a claim on people and things that don't belong to them. They begin to idealize certain people in the world *outside* their immediate family, a family now coming to be spared their manipulation and plunder. The relinquishing of early narcissism is a loss paid for by an initial lowering of self-esteem, and this calls for a kind of rescue operation. It takes the form of stereotyped bursts of idealization that relate now to new people in their outer society.

It is this maturing conscience, in fact, which rescues them in their latency from the loneliness and the depression that goes with their dawning awareness of their fragile ineffectuality. They become buffered by the feelings of self-importance that accompany their new relationships with playmates with whom they can indulge in a communion of interests; here they discover that they can give a little as well as take. The more they reduce their demands on their immediate families, the more they find themselves able to idealize themselves, as well as those others now populating their social world. The fantasy manoeuvre that embodies this ever-flowering conscience is uniquely their own creation, their own individual *family romance*. Where before they were not at all that content with themselves in the developing of this maturing conscience, now they not only evolve some sense of right and wrong, but find that, in their ability to idealize others, they can initiate the desire to live up to the idealized image that they have created for those others.

The main feature of the family romance is an extreme over-idealization of certain new figures in the outer society; such figures are invariably perceived as having a great capacity for rescue — a psychological theme first noted by Otto Rank (1914). This theme could as logically be called a 'community romance'. It is an idealization of extra-familial figures, brought on specifically in early childhood, by the unwanted infiltration of the child's mind with a perception of parents who are indeed not entirely made of immaculate fibre (Helene Deutsch 1945). It signals that the child has developed serious reservations as to who deserves to become invested with the diffidence that the child harbours within himself about matters of a physical nature such as procreation; in this projection, he wishes to share and find confirmation of his own ideals in the now idealized world of figures outside who are to give nutriment and support to his own immaculate ideals. I indicated earlier that the 'primal scene' is the crucial setting round which children first deploy the 'mortar and building blocks' for the walls of their earliest sexual sanctuary — a flimsy structure, yet one passionately designed to remain impregnable from the subsequent intrusive forces of reality.

As the maculacy of genitality threatens to break down the fortress of 'primal scene' mystery, and as children become further exposed to the facts of life as these pertain to their parents, their egos recoil with a disenchantment. In effect, their psyches split. One part whispers that the new factual discovery of conjugal sin is their personal penalty for being unlovable and unwanted children; they feel in this moment of disaster excluded in entirety from the lifeplan of their parents. Yet another part of their egos cries out a denial; this portion aims at a self-restitution from their disillusion. The reduction in the mystique of their parents and the subsequent blow to their own self-esteem becomes softened by an opposing conviction that tells them there are other more 'immaculate' and aristocratic figures in the outer world who surely have retained in totality all the confusions and the spiritual wonderments surrounding the origins of mankind. It is to such figures, still entrenched in mystery, that they must look for salvation; perhaps such loftier people will see their true worth and 'adopt' them. And is it not possible, suggests their fantasy, that they were indeed secretly spawned by less maculate and earthy a parentage than their own? Suddenly a new romance is planted in their psychological lives – the family romance!

The idealizations of the family (or community) romance naturally coincide with a reverse process going on inside children at one and the same time during this latency stage, a process best described as a 'put-down' of all the people in their immediate household. This stage is characterized first by a down-grading of parents; there is little intent to inflict hurt on their elders as the children start in with their unfavourable comparisons; after all, parents too often do very much the same thing to their children. In any event, it commonly begins with the father of your son's friend next door being heralded one day as being 'quite a guy'; your daughter might find this neighbour's wife a 'charmer with cookies'. The process develops rapidly and your child may come up with the real big question, delivered with a straight face, 'Are you my real father or was I adopted?' When it is confirmed that you are, your 'innocent' finds it most difficult to disguise a shadow of unmistakable disappointment clouding his face. I should point out that in the family romance the child's maternal roots are rarely questioned because of the close symbiotic experiences of the infant that capture an intensity not usually attained in the relationship to his or her father.

As young people move out of latency, they do struggle with a certain amount of disenchantment that they feel toward mother; their awareness that she has had something to do in a sexual sense with father is not exactly acceptable to them at this point. For a short burst, the boy especially might even undergo a phase of petulant revenge against mother, it taking the form of abortive research into the area of sex and romance. Drawing upon a vague conception of his father's role in sex with his mother, he might try to impress some of his gang with his biological knowledge. Guiding them through progressive seminars up and away from their theories on how babies come from swallowing watermelon seeds, he tries to bring them up to date on the subject of fornication, settling all disputes by a clinical demonstration in the garage loft. (This usually demonstrates to everyone's satisfaction that he has no more clue what to do than any of his agitated students.)

On the more spiritual level of his relationship to the opposite sex, however, he may be more successful as the little vicarious lover, fighting his cinema heroes' battles and loving their loves; but the lights of intermission will bring him, not the cuddling embrace of the film's beautiful enchantress, but alas, just his plain familiar self — sitting in smelly corduroys, exchanging liquorice nougats and viral infections with his buddies.

Puberty will bring with it objects of infatuation from the real world of the classroom. The young teenage girl might have her football hero and the boy perhaps some unapproachable girl in his school (usually in a higher grade); secretly, he will allow the flames of a developing passion to lick the ground whereon his new love walks. His idealization will consume his waking mind, and the over-valuation of his goddess will distort that little judgment his frail conscience can muster at this point in his life. His love will serve to substitute for some ideal for himself which he is in no way near approximating; he will worship his heroine because of some image which he in no way understands, and his fragile sense of discrimination will become further blurred in this ecstasy. With maudlin diffidence, he might hang around after school to capture from a distance a glimpse of his true love, mooning away his time in a juvenile passion that expresses his willingness to replace (at least temporarily) his own tenuously developed conscience by an outside object. Usually faring a little better at making contact will be the pubertal girl, whose older and wiser football hero might even exploit the easily-won idealizations of an enthralled little 'teeny-bopper'.

THE BARRIER OF THE WILL

Puberty and the years that follow is a period wherein one's early flowering conscience, with its romanticisms and its idealizations, leaves one especially vulnerable to all types of forceful personalities that one encounters in the outside world. Not only does projection continue to operate, but incorporation of idealized outer objects goes on at the same time and with the same intensity as in earlier years. The sense of who one is, or one's identity, is by no means firmly established as yet, and this precariously fragile sense of self naturally disposes the early teenager toward an easily triggered regression, especially under certain provocative conditions such as the loss of a loved one or a disappointment in an idealized object. The result can often be a falling back onto earlier symbiotic attachments to old familial figures. But human development, especially in mid and late adolescence, allows for the development of an intimate set of ego defences to meet the mounting identity crisis of this period of life; these defences — and I talk only about the one most important to charisma — are to safeguard vulnerable youth against indiscriminate choices in idealizations that stem from the strong instinctual cravings for objects during this period.

The particular defence emphasized here has to do with the necessity for developing this sense of discrimination. The need grows for a sense of autonomy (even an illusory autonomy is acceptable) from all authoritative figures in the outer world, and youth is placed under considerable pressure to defend itself against its earlier indiscriminate tendencies. Identity for the adolescent, even for the young adult, demands a special thrust toward emancipation, one that stems from the elemental process of individuation that for human survival starts in everyone's childhood. I have chosen to refer to that particular defence that relates to one's hunger for autonomy or emancipation (sometimes called adolescent rebellion) as the *barrier of the will*. In its construction, the ego draws upon the thrust of the libido that is continuing its search for its way back to the primal love object, and upon the aggressive instinct that is enrolled as well in the fighting for the preservation of that goal.

The barrier of the will is derived from all three agencies of the psychic apparatus, from instinct (libido and aggression), from ego (an inherent emancipatory need for self-control), and from conscience. It is the contribution from one's conscience that I regard as the most significant feature to the adolescent's construction of the barrier of the will. The idealizations of self and outer people not only give object content to our conscience, but value judgments that come to be associated with these idealized persons become separated out from negatively valued objects which then come to be 'dissociated' (split off) from one's conscience and which are subsequently perceived as totally alien. To a large degree then, it is from one's maturing conscience, with both its associative and dissociative discriminatory functions, that the sense of being in *control of oneself* develops (contrasted with the child's feeling of being controlled by others).

It is because of the dissociative elements of one's conscience that one's ever-growing sense of will remains precariously balanced, even into adult life — in fact for all our days. The barrier of the will, like the dikes of old Holland, is far from impregnable; there are natural loopholes and the foundations of the undersoil on which it is built have the quality of quicksand. The spectre of death — one of mankind's most elemental dreads, something over which one has no ultimate control despite man's endless struggle to deny the fact — hovers constantly over the barrier of the will; the struggle is not merely with the literal theme of death, but with another form of 'dying' that becomes associated with this theme — namely with the terror of losing one's self-control (self-determination, freedom, autonomy, independence).

To the struggling adolescent who for the first time begins to experience a sense of self-determination, anything that comes along to threaten this hard-won sense of control, anything even casting doubt on its authenticity, on its structure, or on the validity of its foundations within the barrier of the will, is perceived by the individual as a threat to everything his psychic life stands for to this point. His whole being can become rocked to its foundations; his entire psychological existence is felt to be in jeopardy; forebodings of a living death may accompany any threat to the sense of control. The small child who is accountable to his parent or teacher feels little trauma to his sense of will from such dependency; but for the young adolescent who feels his destiny has been delivered into the hands of an outside agency, such a loss of control is experienced as a living death.

As one moves through adolescence then, a control over oneself, over one's will, becomes the most passionately defended bastion of one's entire personality structure. Society today, as through the years, still expects from youth a strong will, a capacity for self-sustenance, for work, and for an attainment of sexual adequacy that emphasizes the power of the will; on the other hand, it paradoxically threatens youth with serious penalties for exercising that very will. Small wonder that, at mid-adolescence, all authorities become perceived as a major threat to youth. To lose his will is for the adolescent to lose his mind, to lose his very life. Yet in his recognition of the need for a continued nutriment and a direction for the further growth of his personality, he is most susceptible to those 'helpful' forces that threaten to weaken him in the thing he prizes the most, namely his barrier of the will.

THE UNCANNY

I propose at this point in the psychological mosaic to introduce the phenomenon of the uncanny, the excitation of a special feeling of dread, a psychological experience especially peculiar to the adolescent period of life. Not only has it much to do with the paradoxical influences bombarding the barrier of the will, but it also plays a most significant, albeit antithetical, role, as far as this thesis is concerned, in finalizing the determinants of a people's charismatic response to leadership. Freud's thesis on the uncanny (1919) is, by his own admission, open to questioning and reappraisal, and the interpretations and conclusions I have drawn from my own clinical experiences do in fact differ in some measure from Freud's. He approximates most closely my own thinking when he observes (p. 402) that, as soon as something actually happens in our lives which seems to support our old discarded beliefs, we get a feeling of the uncanny. But perhaps a brief resume of Freud's views would be helpful at this point.

He takes the position from the outset that the crucial thing in uncanny experiential phenomena is the feeling itself; as he puts it, it is a problem of aesthetics. He feels that even people with sound intellectual certainty who have surmounted their early infantile superstitions and magical thinking on passions related to death and immortality are still prone to uncanny experiences. The aura of animation given to inanimate objects such as waxworks, robots, life-like dolls, dismembered limbs, or humans brought back to life is for Freud capable of provoking the uncanny by reactivating the familiar castration anxieties of childhood. He emphasizes that the return of such morbid anxieties is a recurrence of something familiar which had become estranged by earlier repression. For him, it is the revival of an infantile feeling on death that gives content to the uncanny experience.

Those objects that trigger the uncanny, Freud observed, are perceived as having an evil quality, both as to motive and to the power they appear to possess for carrying through such evil intent. The uncanny of epilepsy he attributed to the survival of peoples' belief in demonic influences that was inspired by folklore dating back to the Middle Ages and beyond. The effacement between imagination and reality in uncanny experiences Freud related to the accentuation of psychic over physical reality that commonly occurs in the ego of a person experiencing it. He traced uncanny fantasies or dreams of being buried alive to archaic intra-uterine ideas; and the uncanny reactions of many males to the sight of the female genitalia he ascribed to the familiarity implicit in the repressed awareness of one's origins. He is closest to my view in the observation that an uncanny experience occurs either when repressed infantile complexes have been revived by some impression or when the positive infantile beliefs we have surmounted seem to us once more to be confirmed.

Subsequent psychological analysis allows for a reappraisal of some of Freud's themes. His concept of someone 'surmounting' his infantile beliefs is rather casual and does not seem to reflect accurately the tenacity of one's narcissism; the average adult, in my observations, has by no means truly surmounted his infantile beliefs. I suggest that the core of the uncanny experiential state is found, not in a return of old familiar childhood complexes which, though once surmounted, none the less return from their repressed state, but instead in the surreptitious *threat of dissolution to our illusory sense of self-control.* The trigger stimulus for the uncanny is anything that hauntingly reminds us that, though we may have indeed *acknowledged* the reality of death, we have by no means accepted *living* with this reality, other than with understandably narcissistic defences (including illusions of fearlessness, religious passions, and dedications to lofty intellectual and scientific pursuits). I further suggest that this 'demon' trigger agent of uncanny experiences threatening to take away our self-control is none other than a projection (onto some suitable object) of our own terrifying internal image of ourselves, enragedly suspended in a nightmarish twilight of living with the fact of death. In the midst of an uncanny 'visitation', we undergo a deepening of our frailty in our program for self-control and self-determination; we experience ourselves at the mercy of fate or destiny. This recognition we find repugnant, and we set about ridding ourselves of this trauma to our narcissism, this loop-hole in the armour of our self-determination.

For me, the uncanny is a dissociative phenomenon, occurring within the barrier of the will, where one part of our conscience refuses to recognize kinship with another. The uncanny is something familiar which is cast out as foreign. Unlike charisma, it is preserved in this state of total alienation by the barrier of our will, much as a foreign exile, perceived as an alien from the start, is deported and struck from our citizenship. The uncanny is a psychic phenomenon that reflects man's struggle with the processes of his own growth (towards death) and the dreaded feelings that go with such growth. It has an antithetical quality in relationship to other defences (such as, for example, a heightening of charismatic projections) erected by mankind to ward off these dreaded feelings. Uncanny experiences are repetitive, being sporadic and compulsive efforts of man to experience his own death and yet be a live witness to the fact (dress rehearsal). They are 'dying lessons', so to speak, aimed at a mastery over the agony of living with the silent undercurrents of a fate over which we have little control. Norman Brown (1959), for one, has expressed the optimism 'that man could learn to contain death within life' – in concrete terms, to put an end to the Death repression that perpetuates aggression, and to learn instead how to grow old!

Charismatic projections are an antithesis to the uncanny, for they allow idealized objects of rescue to appear in our outer world (in the fields of entertainment, religion, or politics). Even sexual acts, often frenzied, are often used in the service of safeguarding against the uncanny. The various hypnoid conditions, the experience of *fausse reconnaissance* and other mental states induced sometimes by drugs and sometimes by mysticism or meditation, are other expressions of man's recoil from the sinister and creeping paralysis of a visitation from the uncanny. Interestingly enough, though all these phenomena are seemingly antithetical to the uncanny, they themselves carry something of the same uncanny aura. But they represent the lesser of two evils; a partial loss is better than a total loss of control.

DÉJÀ-VU

The illusion or paramnesia of having lived previously through some experience identical to one in our current life is referred to as a *fausse reconnaissance* (false recognition). And one manifestation of this phenomenon that relates to people's perceptions of charismatic leaders is *déjà-vu* (already seen); others are about experiences already heard, felt, and so on. The illusion here is one of reliving a self-same perceptual experience undergone before. It usually occurs at the time of what seems a progressive step in one's life; it is something dredged up to give comfort in the face of some threat, such as a new experience or a move upward or forward. Naturally, it occurs most commonly in adolscence and in the climacterium, especially in those who have a tendency to shrink from a broadening of their horizons (it is most unlikely that explorers and astronauts experience *déjà-vu*).

Adolescents about to move toward adulthood undergo a harking back to their past. Sitting college entrance examinations may not consciously threaten, yet it is a test they never faced before; it is a new experience in which they are judged as fit for a new phase of education. As they ready themselves for this final test, suddenly, for some there is that peculiar feeling: not an uncanny dread, but a sensation that has a certain eeriness to it yet is mingled with an aura of familiarity. The feeling is that one has gone through this final examination before; one is positive about having occupied the same classroom in the past, even though one knows one has never been in the building. Weeks later, while winging one's way on some vacation to a countryside where one has not been before, there again is that same strange feeling: one particular stretch of countryside appears incredibly familiar; a part of one's mind is convinced one has been there before.

The feeling of familiarity offers one assurance that the new experience is not new at all; it attenuates the dreaded element of unfamiliarity. To children fearful of strangers it offers a reassuring protection; 'I have seen this before' is a comforting *déjà-vu* message to the youngster. Anything that threatens people, especially the more vulnerable, anything that gives portent of separation from old dependencies on familiar places and people is most likely to trigger *fausse reconnaissance*; it is a defence syndrome that allows a situation, realistically seen, felt, heard, or experienced as new and foreign, to become transformed by a signal within the psyche into something quite familiar. It is one of the psychic means of controlling time. It lets one temporarily return to the past to avoid new current problems; it allows one to go back in time and place to a re-experiencing of infantile or childhood wishes that have been repressed. In the illusion of suspended time, we are given an opportunity to live through something pleasurable (or sometimes unpleasurable) once again; as well, it offers a sense of support against the unpleasant aspects of separation from old familiar dependencies. In effect, it is another means of creating doubles, of creating a second time round as it were. Like magical thinking and the use of animism, *fausse reconnaissance* assures us that what is finished is not really finished; it is instigated as a means of retaining as much as possible of the earlier *status quo*; at a deeper level, it serves our convictions of an immortal life.

THE STATE OF HYPNOSIS

Freud described hypnosis (1921) as a psychological state characterized by a relative loss of one's function of will, a phenomenon that especially operates in group structures. Freud felt that it was something suggestively transmitted within members of any group, something that could with justice be traced back to the origins of people in a primal horde. He saw the hypnotic state or the state of suggestion as something based not on perception and reasoning, but as a happening that resulted from a neurotic tie between subject and hypnotist. He felt that it was a predisposition solidly founded on something surviving in man's unconscious from the early history of the human family. For this study, the significant aspect in the hypnotic process is that it is yet another example of those psychic mechanisms (such as doubling and *fausse reconnaissance*) aimed at shielding man from his fears of growing toward relative independence; like *fausse reconnaissance,* it occurs in the natural state of development of the human psyche. It is experienced with mixed emotions, since it has some of the qualities of an uncanny experience – qualities which, more often than not, are neutralized by a playful sense of relief from responsibility, and the paradoxical illusion of having thereby acquired a new sense of self-control.

To Gill and Brenman (1959) the main ingredient of the phenomenon is a unique transference reaction, where the subject perceives the hypnotist as an authoritarian figure out of his past to whom he surrenders his will. The tools of the hypnotist are simple; it is a matter of producing limitations on the subject's sensory in-take during the induction phase of the seance, so the hypnotist advises his subject to remain silent and at rest. This co-operative effort by the subject, as with mystical meditation and trance-like seances, carries a hoax-like quality of make-believe and play, and such theatricals, by both subject and hypnotist, reflect the deviousness of man's efforts to weaken and yet at one and the same time strengthen his will: he borrows someone else's imagined powers whilst temporarily relinquishing (to a controlled degree) his own sense of self-determination. Schilder (1953) views the hypnotized subject as being too cowardly to ascribe omnipotent powers to himself and as preferring to attribute such powers to a hypnotist in a masochistic surrender that has somewhat playful overtones. The subject does not take his Svengali as seriously as he does more passionately invested objects, such as a lover or a religious leader.

THE SUBVERSION OF THE BARRIER OF THE WILL

We are now in a position to translate the significance of these phenomena, especially that of the uncanny, into the syntax of charisma. I have proposed that the uncanny is a reminder of the inexorability of life as well as death, an episodic self-admonition that man must live with the knowledge of his ultimate fate. Such a reminder leaves one without any sense of option, consistently contradicting the illusory quality of man-made controls so carefully prepared in childhood, nurtured in adolescence, and futilely clutched in the climacterium when uncanny visitations become more recurrent and more prolonged. Like the sporadic tolling of a bell or the ticking of a timepiece, such visitations are ominous messages from our biological clocks, reminding us of a human metabolism no more within our control than the passage of time.

Despite our inner awareness that we cannot 'stop the world so we can get off', we still thrash about for more autonomy than either conversion, doubling, *fausse reconnaissance*, hypnosis, or meditational trances will allow. It is no surprise that we resort to projection — in this case a projection of the raging robot 'demon' inside us that knows of no complete mastery or control over our fate. To allay the danger of a break-down in our efforts to dissociate ourselves from such an impotent aggressive image, an outside agent is chosen to portray the 'enemy' that threatens all our hard-won illusions of equilibrium, of self-control, of complacent 'surmountings' of the theme of death. By projection onto suitably symbolic and enigmatic objects that are sufficiently estranged and beyond the pale of conscious familiarity, we manage to 'discover' alien monstrosities as suitable triggers for our uncanny experiences. Though each individual has his own pet stimuli for triggering such experiences, there are certain agents that are rather widely shared by masses of humanity. (I have always suspected Freud's personal uncanny agents to be those scientists whom he perceived as constantly at his heels, especially the endocrine investigators who always appeared on the verge of overhauling him with their research into the psychic apparatus. Perhaps they were indeed but grim projections of Freud's own personal biological clock that quietly ticked away its relentless reminder of a life that begged for creative completion.)

The examples Freud offered of uncanny themes and universal triggers include dreams and fantasies in which one is buried alive or paralytically trapped in the clutches of a monster, with no escape. Surely the theme here is one of living in an inescapable situation rather than one of dying. And it is a living without control over one's destiny. Adolescents, as well as people at the climacterium of their lives, have many times expressed to me a feeling of resistance, on one hand, against any further development — a sense of aversion or dread of going forward one day — and a horror of slipping backward, on the other. Their psychic paralysis was associated with feelings of not being in control of themselves; they had an uncanny sense of being influenced from outside. What about lifelike dolls, waxen figures of people, automatons, and robots? Do not these represent images of creatures neither alive nor dead, of things half-alive and half-dead? There are those who suffer from catatonia, whose mental and physical posture resembles something frozen, statue-like, something that captures the physical and psychological state between life and death; and here again, we can detect in the catatonic a theme of having to live with death rather than the theme of death itself. It is a posture in man's struggle for a reconciliation between two facts coexisting at one and the same time: the fact of living and the fact of dying. For many it is an uncanny 'twilight' state.

An external agent, who for one reason or another — whether through religious, philosophic, or political stigmata either physical or mental — qualifies within our conscience as an object capable of arousing our dormant self-doubts about our illusions of being able to control life and death, such an agent is capable of plunging us into the uncanny. In contrast to an object whom we idealize as associated with positivity and self-control, an uncanny agent becomes dissociated from our conscience as a danger to our self-control, an evil and alien force that can only remind us of our fate. It follows that objects linked with the theme of survival in the very midst of death should logically become our agents of the uncanny. Biblical text tells us of the maimed and the crippled and the lepers, people deemed to be beyond physical redemption; they are presented as uncanny. The infirm and the aged of our times, people who have degenerated beyond the capacities of medical reparation, are for many, even now, triggers for the uncanny. The rationalization that society has difficulty in finding means of supporting such people is often a flimsy disguise for the underlying rejection we harbour for the uncanny element involved. Those who have lived to tell of the horrors of mass murder or have emerged scarred from concentration camps or from the horrors of a Hiroshima not uncommonly become tragic agents for humanity's sense of the uncanny rather than objects for mankind's compassion.

Of all the defences that we erect against experiencing the uncanny — and these include the state of hypnosis, the use of drugs, mysticism, and so on — there is one particular antidote that commonly serves successfully to allay our dread. I refer to the charismatic rescue operation. It has to be considered an acceptable, adult-oriented device. It is especially called upon by the growing adolescent in his quest for self-control and self-determination. Illusory though it may be, this particular defence, as worked out within the barrier of the will, favourably compares with other more magically flavoured devices. Yet paradoxically, charismatic rescue operations are, in fact, nothing more in many instances than subtle examples of man's *subversion of the barrier of his will.* Here, in charisma, lies an instrument that not only is used to bring about a projection of one's idealizations, but under certain conditions, a projection as well of one's dissociated and alienated images of the uncanny. In effect, we embrace, at times with a frenzied mania, a charismatic rescue agent whose image not only becomes endowed with our customary idealized projections but is also glamorized by his being selected as an agent who recues us from the dreaded agents of the uncanny.

A charismatic leader then may be chosen to extricate us from the potentially paralytic clutches of a monstrous and uncanny trigger agent, this agent being a projection of the 'demon' inside us that signals that we must live alongside death throughout life. I suggest that certain charismatic leaders have historically been allowed to achieve this double coup, not only vanquishing an adversary but rescuing a people from an agent of the uncanny. Hitler was idealized for more than a rescue of a nation from economic deprivation: he 'rescued the world' from old people, from the infirm, from the insane, from scholars, from Jews — in fact, from just about anyone that could conceivably be a people's projection of that inside 'demon' that repudiates living alongside the idea of death. I suggest too that Hockey Team Canada did more than simply rescue the pride of the Canadian people; it rescued them from the Russian 'Pavlovian' school of hockey which, by its uncanny robotism, made Canadians feel out of control. For many people, their charismatic political choice is a conscious exercise in the preservation of their will and self-determination and a rejection of the forces of coercion and tyranny. In psychic fact, I suggest, a charismatic choice just as often reflects that their barrier of the will is threatened by the fear of the uncanny.

It follows then that the leader who can help people *subvert the barrier of their will* and who can in some way enrol this barrier for his own purpose, rather than challenging it, destroying it, or circumventing it, must reap a compounded charismatic coup. He recognizes not only the stubborn rigidity of this barrier, but he devises means of exploiting that very rigidity by an appeal to its capacities for displacement in the service of defence against the uncanny. He becomes chosen, not as the one who would rob a people of their will, but rather as a supporter who would perpetuate this barrier. He comes as a rescuer of the barrier of the will, but in effect he seduces the conscience of the people. There are instances, I am sure, where charismatic leaders have harboured the worthiest of motives toward the people they wished to lead and have been dismayed by a people's willingness to be seduced. No doubt such leaders recognized that there was little they could do to alter such machinations within the barrier of the will of the mass psyche. It is not far-fetched to presume that they might even have been relieved by evidence that their nation was beginning to recover from such an 'illness'.

Finally, I would clarify that it is not simply the idea of living with death that in itself provokes the dissociation of the uncanny from the barrier of the will. To a large degree, the real 'demon' inside us is the *aggression* that stems from man's inability to escape this awareness of his limitations of control over his destiny. Such aggressions, when dissociated, become duly projected onto the uncanny trigger agent who comes to represent this 'demon'. The epileptic, the insane, the robot – all these provocative agents remind us that, in our lack of control, we are at the mercy of our own reactionary aggressions. It is not surprising, then, that man, in some instances, allows charismatic leaders to offer him a legitimate outlet for all the murderous impulses tied in with this complex, a license to destroy the uncanny agents – whether they be the infirm or the aged, a particular race of people, or scholars and intellectuals – who by their probings might cast some doubt on man's claims to autonomy and control.

For some, the psychoanalyst qualifies as a prime uncanny agent.

THE LOSER

One cannot bypass the revival of one's sexual struggles during the adolescent prelude to charismatic imaging. I have described earlier how the five- or six-year-old develops infantile fears of death that become suddenly enmeshed with his developing sexual fantasies, giving content to his oedipus complex and its associated castration anxiety. The harm, as reflected in his nightmares, that such a child fears is going to befall him relates in fact to a large degree not to realistic dangers in the outer world but to unconscious terrors that are linked to his sexual ambitions to divide his parents and take over the role of one or the other, in bed and out. In the so-called negative oedipal conflict, the girl attempts to displace her father, the boy his mother. The potential for being castrated (punished) is originally perceived by the child as resting in the hands of that parent who becomes the major rival. The child's psyche does not, of course, tolerate this sort of anxiety very well; it becomes dangerous for him to go on day after day living with his executioner prowling about the house. Much simpler for him to displace his anxieties, and it helps him get along with his rival as well. If he is going to have fears, he might as well have them for invented images — mythical bogeymen or witches; even more preferable are household pets like a huge salivating hound that growls so ominously each time he walks by the corner on his way to school.

In adolescence, these complexes re-emerge but with certain modifications. For one, there is a convenient establishment to replace the castrating father or mother (the establishment are figures of authority in the community, such as employers at one's work or university executives whose position of power, among other things, reactivates the oedipal or negative oedipal aggressions). The boy-girl theme makes its appearance in adolescence while some of these immature complexes are still unresolved, and now they become concealed or at least disguised by the 'swinging' braggadocio of this age. The gauche adolescent coming on strong is, of course, going to run into two obstacles right away — his inexperience on the one hand and the revival of his anxieties from the complexes of his earlier period on the other. It is at this age that young people become convinced they are born losers. The young man is reinforced in this impression of himself by the many catastrophes he encounters in his efforts to evolve the 'swinging' image, whether it be the breakdown of his father's borrowed automobile or the ineffectuality of his own penis.

This loser complex will account in part for a rather baffling and paradoxical group choice in leadership, namely of an unsuccessful political figure (as exemplified by one of the recent American presidential candidates) who, while carrying the stamp of a political loser, yet manages to attract the charismatic support of a fair-sized following. Earlier in this book, we looked at the fighting stance in the charismatic image, an ingredient derived from the polarized aggressions of the victors and the victims in a society. Though most of us at late adolescence are realistically losers in our oedipal struggle with a parent, it does not follow that this position becomes compatible with our unrelenting heroic ambitions for an ultimate personal victory. A group, with its numerical strength and a proxy leader to spearhead our frustrated aspirations, will offer an ideal arena in which older adolescents can prolong their personal conflicts in this derivative form of political action.

Those who emerge triumphant from their oedipal struggles tend to resist handing their proxy to any kind of leader, preferring to work toward actualizing their own ambitions. For some winners, the traditional powerful leader may become an object of deferrence — as he might also for losers who feel really defeated. But among other losers who feel more disgruntled or militant or who brood on some vengeful coup, the kind of leader who would appeal would be anarchist or revolutionary and charismatic. There is yet another kind of loser, however, who would choose a loser as leader; such people, some of them professed ideologues, seek in such a leader a vicarious fulfilment of their personal heroics, heroics that depend on perpetuating a fighting stance for losing or even lost causes.

I have set down the egocentric complexes that form the understructure of our psychology: symbiosis, the primal scene, the family romance, the barrier of the will against the uncanny, *déjà-vu*, the state of hypnosis, the loser complex — all these are going to play their part in creating not only our own but everyone else's charisma. They are components of the fertile soil that will ultimately produce and project that particular personality chosen one day to help subvert the barrier of our wills that ordinarily fortifies us against any casual seduction to the past. As we approach adult life, we harbour some vulnerable areas of suggestibility, a matrix of infantile fears and delights that have been shielded by an armour of adolescent reactions and protected by the beginnings of our adult-oriented conscience. At this stage, we are a little tired of our idiosyncratic existence, more than a little fed up with just ourselves. We look for new friendships and we begin to feel the hunger for the group. We are ready to recognize the importance of society and of the social order in granting us a sense of group belonging.

In fact, we are just about ripe for completing our creation of that communal image which is charisma.

Chapter 4

The myth-makers

The time arrives in later adolescence when one seeks to establish some kind of identity in the world in which one lives, in the world outside family, in the world of community. Erikson (1968) has given the label of one's *ego identity* to that which approximates the particular niche in society compatible with one's expectations and self-respect. No longer satisfied to remain but a hodge-podge of earlier identifications with family and close friends, the individual on the move of adolescence begins to crystallize out his own ego identity, a mental configuration of a self specific for him alone. This includes the highest polarity in his identity, his own *ideology*. By ideology, one means a system of abstract ideas which represent some aspect of the reality one desires to live in and to promote which one is prepared to invest some action. One can read from the ideology of an individual much more of that person's character structure than he consciously aims to expose, because ideology is like a dream, a play, or even a neurotic symptom in that each of these harbours its own latent content, its unconscious fantasy, and its expression of the quality of relations sought for with other people. One's ideology is brought about by the elevation and extension of one's growing conscience, in a dynamism that intermeshes and interweaves one's own personal idealizations with those of the community at large.

The quality of one's ideology will vary according to its state of maturation and according to the quality of the individual conscience that precedes it; an archaically vindictive conscience, coloured by the principle of talion and blind morality, stands in sharp contrast to a more mature and communally oriented conscience that flexibly reconciles the more primitive demands of law and order with the forgiving and compassionate elements that are associated with human rights, personal freedoms, and the communal adaptations that allow the individual his particular niche in society. Out of both polarities of conscience, from the punitive (conscience in this context has been often referred to as superego) and from the forgiving (in this context conscience is commonly referred to as ego ideal), comes some kind of reconciliatory ideology with which the individual grapples in striking the ultimate posture he will assume in his relationships with others and the community at large. One's political views, one's religious attitudes, and indeed one's sexuality become ideological expressions of these polarities.

In this triad of human passions, one discerns in any individual the ultimate predominance of his earlier idealizations. An ideology based on the worship of power and physical force, on the subjugation of other people's will, and on the absolutisms of religious, political, and sexual dogmas, all too clearly reflects the underlying failure in that individual's progress toward a reasonable independence — toward an emancipation from the state of attachment that characterizes childhood. Such an ideology fails to disguise the other side of the person's character; the side showing is a profile of dominance, the side hidden is of a person dominated. And the individual harbouring such ideology invariably suffers a reversal to the flip side sooner or later in his life cycle. It is ideology, then, that integrates the successive and partly contradictory identifications of both the individual and the society. It is the expression of the most mature effort by the ego of an individual to elevate the level of his personal ideals to a meaningful relationship to the world in which he lives.

It is a fallacy that one's own individual psychology offers a complete understanding of the group process. The quality of any social organization, though highly dependent upon the nature of its constituent units, is marked with structures and laws of its own, and the sociology of such a structured society can no longer be reduced to the individual psychological components making up this society. However, the converse is also true, namely that theories relating to the behaviour patterns of groups, where only the realities of the social and political forces are taken into account, invariably neglect the individual quirks and foibles of the human psyche that at times precipitate, in the face of all reason, some of the most gross paradoxes in group behaviour. In any event, identity, if one simply thinks of it in terms of individual psychological development, is a rather meaningless idea; without its incorporation into communal structure, there can be no full mature identity, no ego identity.

It behoves us all the more to examine at this point, at least in skeletal outline, the psychological theory on the evolution of group conscience and the origins of human culture. What is the genesis of the group? Are we Darwinian horde creatures with a modern face-lift? Are we the divine messengers of the earth, fashioned in the image of His Being? For those oriented to this latter premise, there is, of course, much less to be questioned on man's evolution; even for those more anthropologically or more scientifically oriented, a knowledge of the evolution of the group process is as scanty and imperfect now as it was twenty or sixty or one hundred years before. Scientists like Darwin and Freud had to use a body of concepts primarily derived from theory and inferences drawn from the study of primitive tribes.

It is necessary to my thesis that I give at least a brief outline of Freud's theory of the primal horde, in so far as his 'great man' will stand in one corner of my political ring to do battle with a revolutionary son or daughter for the charismatic reward of a people. Freud's idea (1913) of a primal member of the species or the father of a primal horde contained the suggestion that individual psychology must have at least originated in pace with the early group process. He points out that over the ages the human race evolved three systems of thought – the animistic, the religious, and the scientific. Animism, the first human philosophy, used as its most important tool the technique of magic, a body of instructions on the attainment of mastery over, or at least some reconciliation with, the chief dread of early man – death. In all ages, mankind has shared an immense belief in the power of human desire; this over-estimation of mental processes is at the root of magical thinking and the belief in animism, a philosophy that endows thought process alone with the power of actions. To primitive peoples, as with neurotics and children, thinking is equivalent to doing. To Freud, man rather than being a herd animal is a horde creature led by a chief; he explains the first group psychology on the basis of the coercive and subjugating powers of a chief overseeing a primal horde of captive followers.

To Freud then, the only person in the earliest days who was permitted to enjoy the luxury of an individual psychology was the chief, the *primal father*. All the other members were seen as tied together in a bondage, whereas the father was free, his world needing no reinforcement from others. Freud speculated that the primal father coerced the sons into a group psychology, where the father's sexual jealousy and intolerance prevented the underling sons from directly satisfying their sex impulses, thus paving the way to his own murder by his sons who, in their cannibalistic incorporation of their father, accomplished their identification with their chief, each of them acquiring a portion of his strength. Freud pointed out the analogy in this theory to some of the historically documented cannibalistic tribal customs. This then was Freud's explanation of the first totemic clan; in the totem feast, Freud saw mankind's earliest festival, a repetition and commemoration of the criminal patricidal deed, and the earliest beginnings of a social organization of moral restrictions – in effect a rudimentary religion.

With the activation of a sense of guilt in the sons, Freud saw the dead father becoming stronger than the living, leading to a renunciation by the killers of the fruits of their victory, namely the freeing of the women that had been kept in bondage. From this filial sense of guilt, he saw emerging the two fundamental taboos of totemism, which correspond to the two repressed wishes of the oedipus complex – patricide and incest with the mother. In the renunciation, Freud perceived a salvation of individual psychological life, which might very well include not only all that one experienced in one's own lifetime, but also all those things present in one before birth – elements of an archaic heritage. Included in this heritage, Freud listed one's primal universal symbols of language and one's primal ideas relating to parents, including the oedipus and castration complexes. He deduced from such a theory that in all mankind there existed a powerful need for an authority who could be admired; he saw this need as a longing for the father felt by everyone from his childhood onwards. This patriarchal image he labelled the 'great man.'

Since the 'great man' image operated in everyone and by virtue of the similarity of authoritative societal figures to the father, there was no need for surprise in finding the role of the group conscience falling to such an authoritarian figure in group life. The assumption of a 'mass psyche' explained for Freud the continuity of the original primitive process from the earliest of man's history down through the years. He saw individuals inheriting certain psychic dispositions which required incentives in individual life to become reactivated. The need of the masses to be dominated by the great man was seen by Freud as springing from the longing for the father, something that lived in everyone from childhood on. In this observation, Freud demonstrated his awareness of a need in people to find their leader in someone.

THE DYNAMISM OF ANARCHY

But just how real an entity is this imaged figure in our contemporary politics? In my view, the great man is not such a part of the fabric of psychological reality as Freud believed. I have already made reference to the fact that Freud's genius in unravelling the mysteries of unconscious processes by no means exempted him from his own expressions of narcissism, an ego phenomenon of all mankind. It is my feeling that, especially in his speculative writings, this narcissism played a significant role in influencing his theories on the origins of culture.

It is, of course, obvious that his suppositions represent a patriarchal concept of human development. For me there is room for strong doubts about this theory — in fact for a gross scepticism. For one thing, any theories pertaining to the early ages of man run the risk of being branded as legend or illusion, unless such speculation demonstrates a clear inter-relationship between the theory and some kind of substantiating evidence in the here and now, perhaps in the form of some imprint that has clearly been left on the contemporary psychology of man. Visible signs or markings in the psycho-politics of our present-day culture that might have their origins in a more primitive era would naturally be most impressive.

Let us reconsider then our present political way of life and perhaps compare it a little with the times in which Freud — and Weber — espoused their theories on leadership. I think few can deny that some things have changed since those times; a 'follow the leader' format for politics was the rule then when monarchy and more or less benevolent autocracy prevailed; people at large were much more prone to behaving like sheep. Revolutionary figures in those times were intellectual elitists, drawn almost exclusively from the student body of the university campuses. Feuer (1969) has offered a conflict between generations as the instrument that dissipated the energies of the unsuccessful German student movement of 1817 following the War of Liberation: none the less, out of a crisis of de-authoritization and disenchantment with the German ruler, Frederick III, and his failures to fulfil the promise of representational government, the German students established a model for the Nazi take-over of a century later. The Viennese student bourgeoisie uprising of 1848 met defeat when it allowed the Imperial party to borrow anarchistic tactics in pitting the revolutionaries against an older generation of the working class and the whole movement spluttered to a halt.

The Russian student uprising of the 1860s and '70s, with its 'back to the people' motif, by its terrorism and the acts of assassination that are so typical of anarchistic uprisings, served to dash the hopes for finalization of a new Russian constitution. Fifty years later, in 1914, a similar anarchistic uprising was to end in self-betrayal among anarchists and a war that brought social collapse to Russia. The same fate awaited the anarchistic uprisings of the intellectuals in the Bosnian upheaval of 1910-14, which also set back for a generation the liberal aspirations of the Yugoslavian peoples. The Chinese students of the same period, though somewhat more successful in that they gave birth to the Chinese communist party, destroyed their own cause by an infiltration of corruption among their own ranks; and from so-called freedom fighters they became authoritarian elitists and dictators eventually coming under the disfavour of Mao Tse-Tung.

Today, anarchistic uprisings are a phenomena by no means perpetrated by intellectual elitists alone; all our youth are involved. Our democracies today not only reflect man's insatiable restlessness for a personal freedom and a wish to be represented in the affairs of his country, but in such restlessness there continue to peep through old undercurrents of anarchistic brooding, which from time to time erupt into shows of violence. Such markings of anarchy, though they have a muted note in the organized affairs of our democracies, are nevertheless very much a part of our contemporary politics; surely they cannot be totally ignored as having no voice in our group dynamics. Their sporadic manifestations throughout the historical development of human society reveal them as forces which must be given their due; they are of psychological significance when we try to theorize in depth on the earliest origins of social structure.

This anarchistic quality in humanity, of dispensing with all leaders, is, I suggest, an undercurrent that makes itself known in other areas than just national politics; it operates as well as an opposing force to anything in our culture that smacks of organization, even organized play. Nor is it a quality shared only by those most active and most vociferous in a community. Earlier, I indicated that one of the character ingredients of the more charismatic image was one of a polarized identity, an active posture in which a side was taken as winner or loser. Now this particular characteristic, this readiness to take a unilateral stand, is a key dynamism that delineates a heroic or charismatic image from, say, the passive imagery of the indifferent society. This heroic partisanship is one essence which activists seem to mobilize in the translation or actualization of their drives, ambitions, and ideologies.

There are many social and personal factors that determine why, for instance, many citizens choose a more passive position in their identification with causes. To my thinking, it is hardly logical to suggest that most of us are simply passive personalities at heart, in direct contrast to the more energetic or the more activist among us. I would venture that the large majority of a population who take a casually passive position in politics are not basically passive personalities in any real sense. Personal choices and styles for living, for one thing, reflect the priorities of one's value systems. For another, many people prefer to activate themselves from behind a wall of camouflage — one of seeming passivity or of ostensibly sheepish docility. Such people are truly puzzled by the energetic boldness of those who 'put themselves on the line' in a bid for leadership. Do you not often wonder, in fact, what strange forces operate in the individual who abandons all the comforts and securities of the peaceful life to go in search of those battles that are so much a part of any political career?

Somewhere in between the polarized stances of activist on the one hand and passivist on the other, there is surely a strong undercurrent in our culture that represents still another stance — a third and intermediary position to which a fair number of people adhere, a psychological posture which can be labelled the 'anarchistic' position. To this group belong those looking for the leaderless society.

Let's examine the anarchistic dynamism as it shows itself, for example, from behind one of its customary masks — a group of the highly partisan 'sports fans' common in our culture. Further, let us focus on one particularly popular sporting event that seems to have lingered on in our society, despite protests that it is an affront to the ethics of a civilized society; many refuse even to consider it a sporting event at all. I refer to the prizefight. The main focus of attention is on the two main characters in the ring — the gladiators, fighting fiercely against each other. We may make some passing reference to the mob of faceless but excited spectators that pay for the arenas and the coliseums of our cities, but very rarely does our interest dwell on those intermediary figures, the anarchists, who might very well be considered from a psychological standpoint neither activists — as are the contestants — nor passivists, as we commonly consider the spectators.

Who are these anarchists? The promoters, for a start. These fringe personalities play a much more subtle yet in many ways more dominant role in the action than the key contestants themselves. The promoters form a very busy entourage of go-betweens and satellites, many of them from the so-called underworld of society. But there may be other anarchists involved as well.

Unlike the coaches or the managers who have a vested material interest in their prizefighters, football players, or hockey teams, many so-called partisans — excluding those heavily caught up in a group chauvinism of one sort or another — may not be quite as they would appear. Some spectators *seem* to identify with one or the other contestant; they assume a surface posture of polarization, having 'placed their bets', so to speak, on a win-or-lose basis; these are the spectators who jump to their feet and make all the noises ostensibly demonstrating an unquestionable loyalty to one or the other of the combatants or teams. In a more subdued vein, there are those who shout instructions and contort their bodies in movements that visibly demonstrate an identification with every movement in the ring or on the field or rink. There are yet others who resemble that breed of teenager who not only is first in line at rock festivals but is most insistent on taking an active part in the proceedings, by fainting or disrobing or employing some other bizarre attention-seeking device that unquestionably disrupts the performance.

One could erroneously conjecture that these zealots were the most active partisan sympathizers of the whole spectacle.

During many a sporting event, people of that ilk have been known to jump from the stands right onto the field of play, then to make public fools of themselves in what appears to be a futile effort at participation. Although the 'fraternity man', of course, could draw upon his state of inebriation to justify such behaviour, yet the fact is that such a participant, intoxicated or not, is obstructing the entertainment, despite an ostensible partisan posture of personal activism. One has to wonder just how many in the stands are sympathetic to such disrupting influences; are they too operating from the depths of a similar psychology, one that represents yet a third faction in 'the big fight'? Is it possible that this wish in people to disrupt reflects in many instances a fuzzy ill-conceived ambition in some way to win the day for themselves — in effect to rid the play of all contestants except themselves?

Let us look again at the promoters who arrange these matches. It may appear on the surface that such an organizing publicity job would be dictated by cold calculated material interests of a quality most foreign to any large segment of a population. Yet the kind of promotionalism that brings two factions or fighters together for the purpose — beyond material gain — of seeing to it that one party 'destroys' another does not call for some unique 'hangman' personality from the dregs of our society. Many of our average citizens, notwithstanding their loud protests, are would-be promoters at heart. I am trying to make the case that personalities, who might be called promoters, represent a fair segment of humanity, not only in today's culture but in cultures that go back to the earliest origins of a group psychology, cultures that hark back to the first nursery of mankind when the primal mother was the pivot of the first group. I am espousing the theory that promoters — or anarchists — have the earliest place in our group psychology, and that they are motivated in depth, to-day as always, toward winning the day by a coup that sets man against man, thus allowing all contestant leaders to be ultimately destroyed in the service of narrowing (eliminating) the competition for the favours of the pivotal mother.

The same dynamisms may be at work in 'the big fight' of a political election. Our first task there would be to find two 'patsies' to fight against each other. Our own personal empathy would lead us to polarize our surface identification and magnanimously allow us to take the side of one adversary against the other. But this would be unrelated to our deeper psychological foresight with which we would prepare for a victory for ourselves, regardless of which contestant emerged as the temporary victor; on the long haul, we aim to be the victors ourselves. How would we accomplish this?

By a process of attrition. Unconsciously, the anarchistic plan is for all contestants eventually to die out or slowly wither away; we, the anarchists, do the 'mop-up job' — technically speaking, a victory through default. As history has demonstrated, great leaders, like prizefighters, often end up in a state of 'liquidation' — and often sooner rather than later. Promoters such as ourselves live on and on.

Most of us, no doubt, like to think of ourselves as quiet peace-loving citizens, spectators of our greatest national sport — politics — ever ready to embrace a victor and to console the loser as he concedes defeat. A startling percentage of the electorate, however, never even bother to cast their ballots. Some of those who abstain from voting are passive people holding little stake in their nations's politics; others who do not show at the polls are expressing dissent about the manner in which democratic principles are being exercised; still others have more hostile reasons for abstaining, such as an antipathy for all leaders and leadership. How many of us are really promoters, I do not know; but I'm sure that many of us are not blind to that element within us that looks for a fight between two contestants other than ourselves. Looking for a fight, I suggest, is one giant step towards promoting one. Do not some people go to political rallies or observe such affairs on television with much the same gusto as (other) people show in attending a sporting match? When we follow the candidates for president or prime minister, are we not looking for some kind of battle, looking for one adversary to 'beat' the other? We're civilized about it, of course, and do not openly lust for spilled blood; and the reality principle has to be served. But none the less, the expression of our polarized identifications in the realm of politics may not be necessarily rooted in demands for a winner or a loser in a fight of hero against man, but in many instances it may be rooted in the ultimate expectation that we the people will emerge, according to an anarchistic dynamism, as sole victors through the attrition of all leaders.

But surely, one might argue, all this anarchy is simply passive aggression. It is like children who want to see a fight between their two older brothers simply for excitement's sake. Perhaps, in some instances, it is like looking for a fight between a parent and a sibling, or between one's father and one's mother, or — now that woman engages in political contests, often explicitly against man and his ways — between brother and sister.

Of course, one can argue that if we go looking for infantile roots, we can find them in just about anything, including politics. But, for all that we should attend to the maturing and wiser aspects of life, including politics and statesmanship, yet we should not blind ourselves to the origins and derivatives, however squalid they seem, of human behaviour. They may serve to warn us of the war-like elements still lurking in our politics, for one thing. And in fact people do use the language of the fight to describe elections. During the Kennedy-Nixon contest in 1960, I was especially struck by the way many people perceived these two adversaries on television: they were much more concerned with the fighting stance of the gladiators than with their ideologies, or with which one showed the greater fear of the other, which perspired more easily, which one 'went for the jugular', which had the greater capacity to put his man away when he was on the ropes. This kind of observation reaffirms, for me, the undercurrent of that thirst for blood that we like to think only applies to events like the prizefights. Many prizefighters have admitted an open contempt for their spectators, or have been publicly angered by the hue and cry from a public that screams 'fix' when a prizefighter fails to put his opponent away. My curiosity has led me to wonder whether most fans look to see one fighter put the other away, or whether just as many at some deeper level want to see both fighters put away!

Has any reader had the experience of witnessing this sort of anarchy in a local organization to which they belong? A leader's authority is challenged by some revolutionary; the indignant parishioners flock to a special meeting, ostensibly either to uphold or to defeat one or the other adversary so that the dignified matters of the institution can continue on their unimpeded course. Yet the deportment of the masses at such a rally gives every indication that many are present in the 'jury box' looking for the 'liquidation' of both leaders. 'Let's have a clean slate! If there's to be a winner, let it be ourselves.'

THE PIVOTAL MOTHER

When one considers the social interplay of the sexes in the present era of feminine liberation, when one recognizes that our present western culture is more strongly flavoured with matriarchal influence than ever before, and when one further considers that there have been sporadic periods in history when matriarchy came to the fore to challenge a patriarchal culture, one cannot help challenging Freud's theories on the evolution of the group. I am by no means convinced of my own speculations and modifications of Freud's theory on culture: yet in the face of the increasing importance of the anarchists and with the increased significance of the female in our culture beyond her importance as mother, I feel that Freud's theory needs questioning.

His concept of the origin of the group rescues the narcissism of the male, allowing him, for one thing, to find refuge in a myth of patriarchy as a possible means of surmounting, or in some way dealing with, an instinctual frustration of mankind that is, in my view, more primary than being imprisoned by a patriarch in an oedipally tainted primal horde. Of all the anxieties faced by man, what more traumatic event is there than his original separation from the earliest mother?

It is indulging in illusion to assume that the so-called 'grown-ups' of our culture are indeed all adults. If we arbitrarily define a state of reasonable independence from a mother as well as a father as adulthood, then are we not taking something for granted in describing ourselves as adults in this meaning of the term? A close scrutiny of anyone's regime of life exposes the fallacy. Most men in their relationship to their wives, for example, demonstrate varying degrees of old infantile ties to their mother. Further, though our cultural communications tend to play up the infantilism of the male in such a dependent union, we find, strangely enough, that there is a more hidden element in many liaisons, wherein the male serves as a sort of mother substitute to his female partner, his role of mother often being conveniently disguised from the awareness of both parties by the fact that such a motherly husband is anatomically and biologically, if not so much psychologically, a male. Furthermore, I think there is something to be gained in speculating as to just how much society has been gradually able through the centuries to substitute for mothers various and sundry communal figures as dispensers of mothering and motherliness. Routine life reveals how one person may continue to play mother to someone else, all in one subtle form or another, the roles being readily reversible in accord with the changing circumstances of the relationship.

The cultural labels given to what could be properly viewed as repetitions of the infantile magnificently camouflage the derivative origins of many relationships. What was once clearly breast feeding and toilet training evolves into various kinds of personal services, such as those provided by waitresses and housekeepers, gardeners, secretaries, and maids. The housemaid is still a significant figure in the way we see the personal convenience of our everyday lives. Surrogate mothers can be of either sex in our culture, and wear a multitude of costumes: as mother's helper, governess, or nurse, as chef or waiter, or as physician or clergyman, 'her' role in whatever garb can surely be traced back to those demands that begin in childhood for a dominant mother whom one could easily enrol, however, in a permanent bondage. One of the prime requisites for qualifying in this role as our public servant is that she or he be warm, obediently courteous, and respectful in the ministrations of her service. From such good-mother expectations is born the 'bad mother' image of the ungrateful butler, the disrespectful maid, the pompous clergyman, or the insensitive physician.

In contrast, then, to the classic Freudian view of a group psychology that roots itself in an original oedipal struggle between a pivotal primal father and his oppressed sons, let us now speculate on another version. It is an anarchistic concept of the earliest phases in the origins of group structure, this time with the *primal mother* as the group pivot. One could postulate a theory about the primitive world, in which man emerged from his mother's womb, a lonely and frightened organism that initially knew only one protection, only one comforting lifeline, namely the body of the mother. To the mind of primitive man, the fear of the elements must have been even more intense than they are to us today. It is reasonable to assume that mothers were then, even more than they are now, the prime objects for their infants and children, for frightened and bewildered fathers would be busy far from their nests, fighting each other and the elements for their own preservation and the survival of their brood. The union of mother and child must surely have represented then, as it still does today, the only tangible hope of an immortality. Further, is it not conceivable that the primal father, a veritable weakling in the face of the power of the elements, had all he could do to look after the safety and comfort of his own nest, sexually and otherwise, without entertaining a harem of concubines?

Given the vulnerabilities of the paternal figure, one might well believe that incest as well as patricide could easily have become a routine phenomenon in the lives of primitive peoples, to the degree that it might well have required the evolution of first an individual and ultimately a communal myth to help the offspring harness these impulses toward murder in their greed for the prized mother lifeline. Out of myth could come the illusory patriarch — a salvage of the fragile status of the mortal and expendable male, faced as he was then and as he still is today with the dangers of extinction in his surface role as the centre of the family. What more logical rescue for the floundering status of the male than a creative imagery of the omnipotent patriarch, emerging out of the narcissistic illusion of the male mind! And such imagery could very well have become acted out on a group level, in accord with Freud's speculations, but as a secondary stage in the group process.

Anthropological and philosophic arguments supporting this approach and contradicting Freudian theory on primal man were presented by Róheim in 1943. Following his studies of primitive cultures still existing in Australia and on the island of Normanby, he concludes that mankind's delayed infancy and prolonged dependency in a colossal struggle against the separation from the mother is the instigating factor in the development of civilization. Róheim sees this trauma of separation as the common bond that unites mankind in group life. At a more clinical level, in the writings of Balint (1960) we find a focus on the origins of omnipotent attitudes, which to Balint have been clinically evaluated on the basis of their being secondary to primary human frustrations. Balint points out that a clinical examination of children and even adults who exhibit omnipotent attitudes reveals such posturing to be a cover for an underlying feeling of an opposite nature, one of a crushing impotence. This thesis Balint has backed up with anthropological data on primitive peoples.

I would suggest that the speculation I offer to counter Freudian patriarchal theory, especially when backed up by Róheim's and Balint's clinical findings, makes it seem logical that we revaluate and interpret further not only the whole question of group mythology, but the evolution of one's own individual fantasy formations as well. In keeping with Balint's concept of a primary love and the mother as the pivotal object, the evolution of communal mythology passed down in remoulded forms through the years might well be analogous to the sequential stages of fantasy development within one's own psyche of the here and now. In both psychic structures, in the individual as well as in the group, one does find a gradual abandoning of certain aspects of the pivotal mother. This abandonment, I suggest, is the motivating factor in the elaboration of one's personal fantasy as well as in the evolution of the group myth of one's outer society.

I offer the proposition, then, that from the sum total of all the egocentric fantasies of the earliest offspring of primitive times, from such children with a common bond (necessary severence from the primal mother), evolves a collective narcissism, an egocentric self-commiseration society if you will, whose group pride continues even to this day to inspire the communal myth of mankind. In my supposition, group psychology has its first beginnings in the nursery, where every child participates in one way or another in an early sibling and clan play evolving out of their temporary abandonment of their mother – an exercise, so to speak, in the expenditure of surplus energy not required for the task of survival. Yet one sees, underlying the play and beyond the attainment of pleasure for its own sake, the early rudiments of a culture and a group process, that affords everyone the time to gain the power and the psychic implements, sometimes through violence if necessary, to find their way back to a total possession of the primal mother.

In the myth of the patriarch, I see the enfeebled efforts of man to harness the violence that goes with such a hopeless quest, a quest never to be fulfilled in reality. In sequence with the ever-widening circle of objects for identification (including the father) within this swelling society of abandoned souls, both group and individual mythology would receive the added nutriment of power, symbolized in the more aggressive behaviour of the male. With play as the cement that consolidated the earliest group structure, how then did such a collection of children, adolescents, and adults come by their patriarchal leader in the dawn of history? How could the theory of a pivotal mother accommodate Freud's version of the 'great man'? Would it not be logical to consider the possibility that the leader, the primal father, evolved as a necessary agent of rescue for all the homesick group members, female as well as male, who shared the common bond of severance from the primal mother?

It is important to remember that the libido of young children of both sexes, as with the aged, is by no means genitally oriented; one need not be critical about the concept of the primal mother as a pivot for both sexes in these particular age groups. Impotent and self-centred people, young and old, might be desperately fearful of two dangers: on the one hand, the elements from without; on the other, their separation from the mother. And the urgency for recapturing the mother would be in direct proportion to the increasing physical and emotional gap with each passing day of relentless separation. One might see such a floundering group looking among themselves, the senior citizens to the juniors and the youth to their elders, looking and groping for power to be borrowed — or invented if necessary. To offset their impotence and to effect the ultimate recapture of the mother would require an extra strength, an extra greatness. And if such greatness was not available in reality, then it had to be created. 'Let us create a great man, from whom we can borrow a variety of strengths, additions, and embellishments that can be expressed both within our individual selves and within our vulnerable group. Let us concoct a group myth that will serve to produce a blend of reality and illusion, from which will emerge all kinds and shapes of leaders for the group to follow and emulate.'

Such a narcissistically motivated patriarchal concoction has long served as a sustaining balm for the corporate ego of mankind, an ego traumatized by the severance from the primordial mother. The omnipotence of the great man reaches its heights in classic Greek mythology: the axe-wielding midwifery of Hephaestus delivers Pallas Athene from the womb-brain of Zeus; the *Eumenides* reveals Acschylus' struggle about the genetic origins of conscience as he attempts to reconcile the age-old dilemma of patriarch or primordial mother as the crucial force in one's conscience. In *The White Goddess*, Robert Graves (1959) deplores Sir James Frazer's condemnation of the Oriental religions (which espoused a communion with God) as the undermining agency of the European civilization of his time; the prime cause of such European unrest, Graves contends, was rather the concept of 'a patriarchal god who refuses to have any truck with goddesses'. A Frazerian 'homage to the welfare of the State', which aggrandizes mankind's anarchistic potency and supreme independence from all objects including a deity, denies, to my mind, the pivotal mother as a hidden passion of mankind, a passion whom man has long feared elevating – even when under stress – to the role of a goddess who might match the powers of the gods.

To offset his impotence and to effect the ultimate recapture of the mother, man turned to a creation of his own mind, his 'great man'. I can visualize the leaders in primitive times as varied in their characteristics as they are today; one can well imagine a different leader one after the other, each taking his precarious and probably short-lived place as chief of the group: one era might have produced the most powerful of brutes, the next one a relatively aged leader with wisdom, a third a virile son, and a fourth perhaps even a primal widow. The acceptance of a pivotal mother for leadership has undergone historical cycles. One could well understand that, in days gone by, the jealous coveting of primal mothers would in all likelihood have posed a more serious obstacle for female leadership than it does today. The present incidence of primal mother figures emerging from their kitchens to take their place on the rostra of global affairs appears to portend an upswing in the cycle, despite the opposition of 'male chauvinists'. Such matriarchal trends in the more progressive and liberalized societies of today appear to hold more promise of sustaining themselves than ever before in history; the logical acceptance of an Indira Gandhi or a Golda Meir by today's democratic cultures implies a quality of greater societal stability than did the matriarchy of the early Amazons or for that matter the reigns of Queen Elizabeth I or Queen Victoria of England.

THE CHARISMATIC COMMUNAL MYTH

If the primal mother is the pivotal object of the earliest psychological yearnings and turnings of the group, we could now identify the two contestants destined shortly to square off in the 'big fight'. I have suggested that out of our communal narcissism comes a creative effort to find someone's greater power to borrow, to find some leader, but a leader who is of necessity expendable in the final analysis, someone to be eliminated by an ultimate liquidation, psychologically or physically induced. After all our gladiators and combatants have paired off right up to the 'big fight' where one will 'knock another's brains out', it will be the people – the anarchists among us – who will find our way back (so we would like to dream) to the primal mother. I suggest it is ourselves, the promoters, the lay public, that we look to see as the real winner of the 'big fight'. It has for years been necessary to create myths that camouflage this element in the psychology of our politics; to this end, as we have in the past, we continue to identify our gladiators as kaleidoscopic images of different leaders. In one corner, then, we are certain to see the world champion, the 'father', the member of the establishment; in the other corner we'll have the 'son' or 'daughter', the revolutionary figure, the charismatic hero! But in the final round it will in depth be ourselves, the people, going against any leader, because in the end we intend to outlast any and all of them.

My theory both resembles and differs from classic Freudian theory on the origins of the group: Freud pits the father and the son in opposite corners of the ring for his 'big fight', an oedipal victory for one or the other: my version is seemingly identical except for one important issue: the oedipal contestants come not from the stuff of reality but from the communal myth of a patriarchal culture concocted by man to assuage his profound sense of underlying impotence – an endlessly surviving mark of an agony he underwent in his rupturing separation from the body of his mother.

The female reader might well consider this thesis to be every bit as male-oriented as Freud's. My position infers that the female in our society (like the male) is, in depth, primarily tied to her mother, and that her heterosexuality is purely a secondary displacement of libido onto the father and his substitute figures. I can only say that my clinical findings appear to corroborate this state of affairs. But let me add that, if one recognizes mother attachments in the female as basically pregenital (not oriented to genital sex and procreation), then the more nutritive attachment that everlastingly survives between woman and woman is to my mind less implausible a concept.

The group or communal myth is then a collective creation of mankind, stemming out of a group narcissism, out of man's awareness of the necessity for severing from the primal mother; yet at the same time the myth permits him to retain the hope of finding his way ultimately back to that object; as such, it occupies a 'twilight' position somewhere between dream and waking reality. Like its pathway through history, the communal myth is an endless, never-completed story, reflecting the conscience of each successive generation, its cultural standards, and its ethics. In the evolution of communal myth, talented and creative persons, whose acute perceptions of their own desires and inhibitions can rightfully credit them with the significant role of the myth-maker, revive a story moulded and worked on through the generations, embellishing and altering it to keep pace with the times, so that it eventually emerges onto the current media of communications with all the freshness and the bloom of a new and virginal creation. The date stamp of the vintage is always there, discernible by all those who would see. Each era brings its own bottling of myth, its own elixir whose content has its own 'expiration date'. It becomes a special form of shared experience, wherein the individual is brought into communion with those of his cultural group on the basis of a common need for love and rescue. Just as one observes in children and in oneself the successive waves of fantasy that reflect one's growth and development in the struggle with one's narcissism, so too one can discern the same sequence of layers spread on down through the years in the serial embellishments of the communal myth. This very passing down from generation to generation, this historical heritage, is what gives the essence of communality to the myth, as contrasted with one's own private individual fantasy, shared only to a degree by one's smaller family group. Yet just as communal myth carries some of the flavour of one's own individual fantasy, so do one's fantasies reflect the same theme as that of communal myth, an inexorable interweaving of the two forms of creativity.

Television script writers, among the prime myth-makers of our culture, offer the images, the words, and the music to our common fantasy. All those stereotyped 'epics' that come into our homes every night of the week are the very essence of the modern communal myth. Every era has brought its own anti-sociality and its own reform, and the media of each era keep pace with the climate of the times. The theme of animism continues to be exploited to the hilt. In the past, we lived through the adventures of Superman as he transformed himself from spectacles to flying cape in magnificent animism and in endless struggle with the forces of evil; then there was the 'lonesome cowboy', arriving from somewhere accompanied by his misfit companion, sooner or later putting things in order before disappearing into the same blue nowhere whence he came. Aimlessly galloping about the countryside in repetitious camera shots of the same rocky stretch of low-budget scenery before finally rescuing the oppressed from the treachery and villainy of 'varmints', he would at the close always canter off into a western backdrop, stoically resisting the sensual smile of an adoring school-marm; the ending only strengthened our group awe for this masterful celibate; what a man to repudiate his instinctual passions in the face of such overpowering charm!

The emphasis on our communal hero of today has shifted to glamour! We need only sit for moments on an evening before the TV set to be confronted with the omnipotent hero of our times. One of our favourites might now be the trouble-shooter, 'the private eye'; or a freelance journalist caught up in international intrigue; or a 'defrocked' police-man in each serial episode out to clear his name in one way or another. In each and all shows, you can bet on it that your man is unattached, encumbered by no one, independent, always alone! He appears first from out of nowhere from a *foreign* city! Though his origin from the primal mother is implicit, his paternity is unknown; he is the self-made man. He walks the city streets a solitary and lonely figure, munching on popcorn and looking for trouble (he is *severing* himself from the mother's breast, yet ready to fight to retain this primal object). Your hero then is a stranger, a foreigner, at this point outside the nursery group, but more than ready for the *play*, primed to indulge your communal fantasies, prepared to introduce you to your parental substitutes and sibling rivals. Now he has a 'sister': he's communicating with her by intercom from his car; he calls her his 'girl Friday' — every private eye has a girl Friday (slave or maid). So he's not alone anymore; next, he's sprouted a power symbol — a phallus (a long sleek car). Things are beginning to hum: revving up his four hundred 'horses' to the background music of a massive orchestra suddenly produced out of nowhere, your hero carries with him a pulsating rhythmic blend of aggression and libido; in shiny mohair, with unfastened foulard, goggles, and slight growth of beard, he moves into high gear, thrusting his long-hooded and narcissistically inflated sports-phallus into the crisp air of the city night.

Now he's in his big office, and with his girl Friday. Naturally, she too is a foreigner and she's damaged — she's black! She has an ethnic *stigma*. (In other such vehicles, girl Friday might be a social worker — with a limp.) She is an object of inherited social significance. Occasionally, some of the bolder scriptwriters have experimented with a Jewish girl Friday or even a North American Indian squaw. In any event, the sociological message of a war against prejudice and against the taboos of inter-racial sex is doled out in these epics in liberal portions. We even discover that girl Friday (maid, mother) is the ideal secretary — faithful, diligent, and stupid.

Time now for the various images of the *primal father* to appear. In keeping with a theme of duplication, you suddenly see father figures crawling all over the place. First, you have your private eye's subaltern, in this instance not the grizzly and toothless figure of the western, but a rotund buffo type whose moronic actions offer a combined devaluation of father as well as the comedy relief in such mirthless extravaganzas. Yet another father misfit is the local police inspector, a bumbling old fool who has failed to solve one crime in his twenty-six years of tenure. And there's the universal father image — the victim! Only his name actually appears, a name spoken in whispered reverence; the script naturally calls for this oedipal father image to be played by a corpse (a victim of murder, eliminated right off from claiming the mother). It's up to our private eye to rescue us from our guilt (we are all of us the murderer), to expiate our sin, and to make restitution for our communal crime. So that the murderer may be suitably portrayed as a man ostensibly cloaked in innocence, a man in white is introduced – a doctor; the patient (father) was given a lethal dose of anaesthetic – purposely. A good script would provide some flashbacks of a cardiac oscillograph sputtering to a halt and an anaesthetic bag, totally deflated, would be caught by the eye of the camera. The horror of animism grips you: is father alive or dead? Was there a respiration? Was there a twitch? It's *uncanny*.

But the father is indeed dead. Our hero must redress a wrong. The *oedipal* theme calls for justice! It remains for our private eye to manoeuvre his way through a series of undercover hide-outs and nightclubs before the villain is apprehended, caught in the act smooching with a chanteuse in a bar (the *sexual* mother, a slut). There's a fight. The villain is never in himself a match for our hero (our omnipotent self), so additional thugs are introduced to give our hero (and us) an inordinately savage beating (further expiation of our communal guilt). Our hero, looking as if he's been run over by a truck, is picked up from the gutter by the bumbling police inspector who laboriously conjectures that 'there's been some foul play'! In the next scene, we're assured that castration is by no means complete: our hero has but a slight smudge (charismatic *stigma*) under one eye, accentuating the *magic* of nature and the indomitable spirit of man.

At last, the murderer is brought to heel and, true to contemporary reform on capital punishment, is rarely killed off, meeting instead the due legal process of a forgiving but cautious society. Only occasionally do residues of the more vengeful past rise up and the villain is permitted, by accident only, to fall off a steep cliff and so make his inauspicious exit. Sociological progress is a major theme in communal myth. The idea of a new breakthrough in man's relationship to man and man's relationship to woman is generously sprinkled throughout any given episode. In keeping with the new social freedoms, our private eye is often cast as a man of

questionable integrity; in occasional versions, he is a man
with a prison record, albeit innocently accused. And a new
myth replaces the already outdated one of the asexual hero;
sexual man finally replaces the celibate. Our streamlined hero
is the prototype of all things related to money and sex; in
fact, he may openly admit he is in business 'for the buck'.
Here is progress and a new courage. Gone is the cowboy
hypocrite who redresses wrongs for the sheer sake of
decency. Today our man is no longer above 'making a pass' at
a woman. There is hardly an adventure series today, on
television or in film, where the contract does not call for hero
and primal mother symbol to be found in bed together: the
camera moves in to show them naked as the day they were
born, and in full keeping with the sexual revolution the
woman should be on top of the man (primal reunion and the
interpenetrating mix-up of Balint).

The communal myth aims to keep our own chances alive
forever. Hence our hero, like the villain, never ends up with
the woman. In the end, he must return to the same lonely
city street, munching on the same popcorn; just as he first
entered from out of nowhere, so he must return to the same
fate. In keeping with his omnipotence and immortality, he
will revive himself in the next serial, and the next, and the
next — always toying with danger and always in the end an
oedipal success who never quite wins the prize for keeps.

Chapter 5

The quest for a niche in society

As we move through late teenage toward early adulthood, we carry the markings of our own personal family myth that has become clustered around the nucleus of our archaic heritage and its organic roots. By this time we are already gathering the earliest overlay of embellishments of shared communal creativity that will come to date us and identify us with the times in which we live. To this youthful and still growing period of our lives we dedicate an excessive energy, which we are more than willing to invest in our zealous and enthusiastic search for an ego identity and a niche in society. Until this quest is either reasonably fulfilled or sufficiently frustrated by an outside world, we are not, at this point, prepared to resign ourselves to the proxy of an outside hero as champion of our ambitions for ourselves.

Involved in such a quest for our own niche is our preoccupation with value systems, wherein the options available are as varied as they are transient, shifting rapidly from those related to sexuality, love, and procreation, to those tied up with the physical prowess that goes with the aggressions of war or the combat of sports, or shifting from those ideals involved with work and the achievements of work to the options of material reward or to the intellectual persuits, or from the attainments of ideological station to a value system that relates itself to the elevation of cultural, artistic, and creative standards. Sometimes we even exercise an option motivated largely by the blind quest for a fame or a notoriety. Whatever the options or values chosen to give content to our ultimate sense of ego identity, it must become a value system that requires a continuous input of that nutriment afforded by both our individual and communal environment to which we are born, develop, and adapt ourselves in our later years. Ordinarily, we seem to choose our friendships, our marriage bonds, and our everyday pattern of living in accord with the inspiration afforded by those who have customarily shared our own value system. From such influences we develop our *social character.*

On the question of what brings about socialization in humans from their infancy on, Freud (1921), in keeping with his thesis on the origins of groups and his emphasis on the role of aggression in early group psychology, expresses the qualm that it is not an easy matter to trace any skein of social instinct in mankind. He points out that nothing in the nature of such an instinct or group feeling can be observed in children and that such a seeming herd phenomenon only begins in reaction to the initial envy with which the older child receives the younger one in the early nursery experience. In consequence of the impossibility of the child maintaining his hostile attitude without damaging himself, he is forced into identifying himself with other children, as Freud points out. The first demand made by this reaction is for justice, namely equal treatment for all. If one cannot be the favourite oneself, then at all events nobody else is to be the favourite. Here in a demand for equality originating in one's earliest envy at the sibling level, stands the Freudian root of social conscience. For Freud, social feeling is based on the reversal of what was first a hostile feeling, one that becomes moulded into a positively toned tie in the nature of an identification; such a demand for equality in the group, Freud points out, applies only to its members and not its leader.

In contrast to this argument and in keeping with the alternate theory wherein the pivotal mother plays the key factor in group psychology, I would propose that a quest for a group identity may be neither motivated nor mechanized, as Freud has suggested, purely by the common bond that one harbours with his fellow in relationship to a leader. For me, socialization is strongly coloured with a necessary dependency of an individual on his fellow toward a strengthening of the fragile ego he retains into adolescence and even adulthood. As he grows, he requires others to afford him power and to share his workload, even as he struggles in his quest for some autonomy; he also needs others for the corroboration of his developing sense of reality, this being no trivial task, but rather another hard-won ego achievement. Everyone yearns for a sense of independence sooner or later, including a wish for an individuality of thought and emotion. Yet despite this hunger for our own originality, there is for us all a sense of comforting confirmation in the discovery that what we have conceived as something of our own happens to be shared by others with similar original ideas who are also 'special', who have also been 'called'.

The structure of the group in today's democratic society does none the less demonstrate that many of us do not remain subdued in a docile abdication from hopes and ambitions for some kind of unique hierarchical status. In keeping with Freud's sentiments on the matter of social envies and hostilities, it is demonstrable in our culture that a struggle for some kind of prestige, for an individuality that might lift us to a degree above the throng, leads us in a quest for causes that will fortify us against the persuasive influences that threaten to submerge us within the massive anonymity of a group bondage. I would point out that many of us carry the residues of these unfulfilled causes into our adult lives as well, left-over imprints of our very early strivings for a more elite identity within a group and even of an undying yearning in some instances for more ambitious fulfilments, such as displacing one leader or another.

Despite the efforts of the modern society to steer people towards a classless system, it can be observed that the earliest roots of both individual and group psychology are still at work in fostering a nutriment for the thrust that pushes us towards a class identity of one sort or another. As far as I can make out, this continues today in our nurseries, in our grade schools, and in our adolescent and adult societies as well. The differences in a child's grades, for example, still represent a significant status symbol for his particular niche in society. The area of the theatre and the arts as well beckons the more dramatic efforts of a youngster's quest for a niche. One need only attend an annual community display of local amateur ballet to witness the process. On the surface, the over-all message of such an exercise is the importance of *esprit de corps* for group participation; yet as the evening unfolds, it is more than apparent that, whatever the individual short-comings of the cast, there throbs within the underdeveloped bosom of each dryad on the stage an unquenchable passion to be one day a prima ballerina — to have a niche in society!

It is not the child alone who strives for recognition through such artistic channels of expression; there is, as well, the undying yearning of the charismatic ambitions of elders, still in search of their own ego identity. Before grudgingly settling for a stranger to play out and rescue all the frustrated hopes they held for themselves, parents, grandparents, and teachers tenaciously hover in the wings as their youthful marionnettes respond on stage to the strings of these parental puppeteers.

RCMP: SYMBOL OF NATIONAL IDENTITY

In our adult society, despite the fact that class distinction is now more than ever considered undesirable, exclusivities and snobberies of one sort or another linger on. Though there have been attempts by some politicians to replace status and class with a more liberal-minded just society and a higher spirit of democracy, there is still strong evidence that, the fewer the other reasons an individual has for maintaining his self-esteem, the more tenaciously he clings to his archaically rooted symbols of social status. The intensity behind the struggle for such status suggests that class distinctions have been invented for some other reason than for power alone. I propose that they are charged with conflicts that centre around a sense of measured self, around the image of one's ego identity, especially one's national identity.

It is somewhat a paradox that from the frailties in the sense of one's personal identity springs the very force of those strivings which give fibre and cohesion at a group level to an individual's entrenchment in symbols of national origin. And it is a familiar fact to everyone that many a misfit citizen, floundering in a morass of personal ineffectuality, suddenly finds himself a veritable pillar of strength when caught up in the passions of some 'old school tie' cause. Many Canadians, for example, whether of the eastern, central, or western provinces, have retained in one degree or another, the same omnipotent flavour in group imagery that their ancestors enjoyed in the days when they were part of a real monarchical system. Some are as reluctant to abandon this pipeline to a royal national heritage as they are averse to giving up the rituals and the symbolisms invested in their religious traditions. The cry not too long ago over the abortive efforts of the Trudeau government to drop the letters RCM from the RCMP (Royal Canadian Mounted Police) is a case in point.

Some of our citizenry still wonder just what the fuss was all about. For one, there was the matter of a government tampering with the organicity of a nation, an intervention which many deplored just as they would have repudiated the bumbling efforts of a psychiatrist or a clergyman proselytizing the adherents of another following. Second, there was the factor of tradition in general being challenged by innovation, a social phenomenon that through the ages has stirred up all the usual counter-reactions from those entrenched in those traditions which represent for them a stable national identity. Further, there was the matter of party politics: the right-wing Conservatives were obliged to maintain a posture that branded any abrupt change wrought by the Trudeau government in the matter of national symbols as a direct threat to the not too robust Canadian identity. On still another level, and perhaps the more interesting one from a psychological standpoint, there was the element that related itself to the individualized and to the mass unconscious of a nation's sense of pride and conscience. On this level, there could be discerned a diversity of emotional responses in the Canadian people that reflected the variety of crises which all citizens experience on their tortuous odyssey for both a personal as well as a national niche in the larger society.

To elaborate on this deeper element in the mass psyche, let us speculate for a moment on the particular posture the Trudeau government assumed in the RCMP affair. To begin with, we have no proof as to exactly who instigated this attempt to tamper with a national symbol; we do, however, have good reason to conclude that someone in power condoned it. It is logical then to suggest that those in the Liberal government suffered no undue sense of either personal or collective loss. Why then was the Trudeau government so emotionally prepared and many others not? Was it simply because of a Francophile readiness to promote the downfall of traditional symbolic ties to a British mother-land, an expression in effect of their basic sympathies with or fears of a Quebec French nationalism and its envy and hatred of things Anglo-Saxon? Or is it that the Liberal government represented mature leadership, not only secure in the personal ego of its leader Pierre Trudeau, but philosophically ahead of our times, a government that was to guide a people from an abyss of infantile dependencies into a new and exciting world of autonomy from an outdated mother-country complex that has embraced two mothers? Perhaps it is simply that Pierre Trudeau had 'arrived' and that the rest of the country had not; conceivably its corporate spirit may have been to some degree willing, but its flesh far too weak.

No political posture could be more clearly identified as an opposing polarity than John Diefenbaker's pronouncement on the RCMP affair. His message was predictably in keeping with the patriarchal 'great man' image that he has traditionally represented. With his profound sense of organicity, Diefenbaker perceived efforts to expunge the RCM as attempts to 'emasculate' the Canadian police of its heritage of conscience.

Now no one would be puzzled as to why many Quebec nationalists and perhaps Canadians of other ethnic origins would prefer dropping this and other symbols of Canada's deference to a British motherland, but let us focus rather on the psychology of the symbolism and inspect this from the theoretical premise that the origins of the entire population of Canada were in fact derived from the United Kingdom; for even under these conditions, a matter such as the RCMP affair would still be charged with emotional turmoil. There would have been the same major upheaval between traditionalists and those for an 'Independent Canada' just as surely as there will be another furore in the not too distant future.

To get down then to what is involved, one can see firstly that Diefenbaker's accusation of emasculation reflected his perception of the power and the muscle of a police force as something more than an agency of law and order. The RCMP represented the nation's potency — indeed its very conscience (something derived from the archaic roots of a nation's organic heritage). The parameters of the Diefenbaker indictment are several: the RCMP is clearly for him and his followers a traditional symbol of the country's identity and values. Implicit is the theme of a rugged perseverance (the Mounties always get their man) and a dogged pioneering spirit (the machine age fails on all counts to replace man's loyal friend, the horse). Further the word 'Royal' has obvious connotations (commoners are to be assuaged that at least their police are royal; citizen A may be an insignicant speck, but he can derive solace from the knowledge that the communal conscience of his country is still born from kings and queens). The c in the emblem signifies that a 'Canadian police' is vastly different from simply 'police'. Herein lurks a condensed disavowal of foreign emulation; the implicit message is that Canada will never dissolve into that oblivion that would equate the Canadian conscience with the non-descript *polizei* of a banana republic.

Lest any deride the indignation of Canadians reacting against a threat to their insignia, let me suggest that they too would be similarly outraged were any of their root symbols threatened with extinction by a fast-paced progressive government. Imagine the repercussions if the FBI were to be changed to the XYZ, or Scotland Yard to Ireland Foot. Conjure up the fleur-de-lis of old France transformed into a 'blade-of-the-cactus', or an 'Uncle Sam Wants You' poster reading 'Aunt Nellie Wants You', or the Star of David replaced by the 'Sign of the Bagel'!

This is all child's play and image-making, the sophisticated citizen may exclaim. This petty symbol business is what makes our country ail! It is long overdue that we move ahead, surmounting these infantile anachronisms and abandoning the inflated escutcheons and the monograms of a national pride. Let us grow up; it is time for the mature classless society! But is it? Is there ever a right time for a nation — or an individual for that matter — to divest itself of those symbols of its origins? My earlier thesis on the roots of identity and conscience stands in opposition to those who would claim that independence (individual or national), even from one's early ties, is ever won by placing geographic, temporal, or symbolic distance between the would-be emancipate and those early objects. Adulthood is marked by a security of self that allows one to remember and to acknowledge both the worthy and the unworthy aspects relating to one's roots. The adolescent, like the child, precociously attempts to become self-made by an amnesia, by changing his fingerprints so to speak, by self-inflationary symbolic pronouncements of independence. One can well empathize with a youthful nation such as Canada getting tired of its growing pains, and wishing, like the adolescent, to shake off the embarrassing stigma of a national flag that suggests the idea that all Canadian citizens are still children reporting to a parent across the sea — a colony of infants boarding out abroad. However, this does not alter the psychological fact that the latest Maple Leaf flag neither changes the national identity nor the state of Canada's realistic independence or lack of independence. Neither a flag nor a police symbol can effect the completion of a nation's processes of maturation.

In the two opposing views on national symbols, the RCMP affair brings into focus the romantic polarities of the communal heroics of a people. But though Diefenbaker's view may well be a classic patriarchal concept that symbolizes the conscience of a Canadian society as something Royal (omnipotent), Canadian (not Methylranian), Mounted (a shiny horse-powered phallus), and Police (a national conscience that is derived from coercion), nevertheless implicit in the accusation of 'emasculation' is a stern rebuke to those who believe one grows up when one stops writing to the folks at home. Even those who wish to assuage a people with an idea that they don't believe in themselves — especially at the national level — are, according to my logic, indulging themselves in a condescending and bribing tactic, like the feeding of candy to a baby.

The Trudeau government's position with respect to symbols illustrated the polarity of charismatic innovation. In this position, national conscience comes not in any way from its royal national tie to old moorings, but ostensibly from an emancipation from all primal attachments. Though on the surface at least, this position might appear mature — a progressive move towards the just and the classless society — yet when one takes a closer look at the politics and the timing of this move, one is left with the realization that we were dealing either with a deftly diplomatic but futile effort to smooth the ruffled feathers of French Canada (or other ethnic groups) or with an unfortunately precocious effort to convince a Canadian citizenry that national independence is easily attained by undergoing 'plastic surgery'. Perhaps this manoeuvre was a reflection of our politicians' perceptions of Canadians — individually and collectively — as being unsure of their own adult capacities, and willing to have recourse, from time to time, to annihilating symbols in an effort to claim sole authorship of that part of their conscience (royal) derived from their ancestry. Like the bolder Catholic who can emancipate from fish on Friday, like the Englishman who can get along without Yorkshire pudding, or the Irishman without his stew, so did the Trudeau government hope to transcend the Royal Canadian Mounted.

Perhaps the only significant psychological issue in this area of national symbols — flags, emblems, or police cruiser monograms — is the degree of unresolved passion that seems to remain as a measure of Canada's vulernable sense of identity. The agitation of the people only brings home all the more powerfully the underlying fragility of many an average citizen's sense of national self. The actions of political leaders only further confirm for us these human frailties of Canadian identity. I doubt that many really believe that symbols will ever profoundly affect the vital functions of a nation one way or another. Emasculation is surely not the anchor issue. What happens if you remove the bagpipes and the kilts from the 'Ladies from Hell' — do you really annihilate the fighting capacities of a Highland regiment? What happens if you take the 'f' out of 'fuck'?

What is at stake here is one aspect of a national self, especially the abstract yet significant sense of one's acknowledgment of the historical past. It appears, therefore, that neither of the romantic polarities of our country's leadership was accurate in its appraisal of the Canadian condition. The Trudeau view demanded of an adolescent nation the emotional posture of an inveterate old-guard emancipate; the Diefenbaker view continued to perceive the Canadian citizen as an infantilized organism whose bathings in imagery represent his main source of national identity. Neither position captures the psychology of Canada, a nation in flux, one that demonstrates the paradoxical polarities and mood swings of an adolescent in mid-stage rebellion against ties to the past.

Somehow the effort of the Trudeau government over this symbol can, when examined closely, be no more vindicated as a step toward national independence than can the consternation of those crying 'emasculation'. The Trudeau government's ultimate retraction of its position on the RCMP affair would indicate that there were sufficient Canadians opposed to tampering with symbols, and strongly attached to that part of the national conscience derived from ancestral roots. Furthermore, it is not deflating to our national sense of growth to conclude that the solidarity of Canadian identity does in some measure depend at this time on the symbolism and traditions stemming from such roots. Until it truly develops the national ego that can allow it a more casual option on its symbols, until it has fully 'arrived' functionally, a healthy Canada will not be formed by reactionary adolescent tamperings on the one hand, or by an exaggerated protective homage to ancestral symbols on the other. The signal of Canada's arrival at adult national status will be marked by its equitable and appropriate acknowledgment — without protest or undue allegiance — of all those mother-country symbols that mark the ethnic roots of its population.

THE ACTIVIST

The quest for a more individualized niche than one of national heritage and group pride takes on political overtones on the day the individual leaves high school, if not before. Whether he goes on to a higher education at a university level, there to become steeped — willingly or unwillingly — in campus politics, or whether he takes his chances for better or for worse in the outside world as a tradesman or a labourer, a member of the unemployed, or a cog in the armed forces of his country, he soon becomes swept up by the politics of some group. Whatever his choice of vocation, he quickly comes to recognize his social status in that group — namely a subordinate. Whether he likes it or not, there, immediately above him, sits a chief — a man or a woman who possesses superior status. Like the chiefs of all cultures from the earliest of ages, our chiefs of today are perceived by their subordinates as being possessed of a power that their underlings do not have. In primitive times it could mean death to any subject who addressed his chief directly; an intermediary, however, of lesser power than the chief but of greater power than the subordinate, could approach the leader unharmed and could in turn be approached by his inferiors without danger. The divine person who epitomized the corporate life of his group was perceived as a source of danger as well as a blessing; he was not only guarded but he was guarded against. His sacred organism, so delicate that a touch could disorder it, was deemed to be charged with a magic which could have fatal results to those with whom it made contact (see Frazer 1890). The same magical power affords us in our times as well an index of our social station – albeit without the penalty of death.

This hierarchical power endows a person with a status distinct from any religious or moral framework and can be described as something that imposes a certain taboo on its possessor. An underling on the student council of a university campus, squeamish about contact with his chief because of his hostility and envy of that chief, will avoid dealing directly with his superior, whereas he will not hesitate dealing with someone immediately above him whose position he envies less, a position possibly attainable by him in his immediate future. The smaller the difference between the amounts of status possessed by any two officers of the group, the less such a difference provokes envy in either of the two parties; the power and the status differential between a chief and a vice-chief of a group presents less of an ambition-provoking stimulus to the envious vice-chief; it is also less of a cause for the chief's own insecurity than is the power differential that exists between the chief and some more remote underling further down the ladder. The conflict experienced by one of the more ambitious members of a group making his bid to move up to the very top is often resolved by his acquiring an intermediary station which, though bringing only a partial fulfilment, yet spares him all the dangers that go with the kind of ambition that is satisfied with nothing short of reaching the pinnacle.

Those with an especially strenuous ambition to reach the very top should remember that many such have been wrecked by success! Not only is there always the problem of a sapping of energy that comes with such a lofty aspiration but, perhaps even more significantly, there is always the element of old unresolved expectations of disaster (castration) for daring to challenge the man at the helm (father). For the adolescent especially, with his first tug into a full group psychology, climbing to contest the very top position often gives him cause to exercise a restraint, especially when he first recognizes the fear and the hostility from the man on high and the seething envy of his fellows below. Small wonder then that so many quickly catch on to a compromise and happy solution — an intermediary position.

This kind of ambition has created a social entity in our politics that can aptly be labelled the 'right-arm personality'. On the surface, it might appear that such people have come into such a category purely through the wheels of political machinery: closer scrutiny reveals many are right-arm by choice. Such a position has given them a sanctuary and a vantage point that allows them the freedom to aggress against the chief at every turn of the wheel, and at the same time enjoy a smug well-liked status where they can hold at bay all the wolves below howling for the top man's hide. The social deportment of such a happy right-arm is a dead give-away; this man is full of quips; he is the group clown; he feels safe enough to well afford this euphoria. With little responsibility, he is approachable as an intermediary from all sides; comforted in the conviction of being well-liked, he can if he chooses even entertain the glittering possibility of one day achieving the very top — through the defeat, the default or even the eventual demise of his chief; and under such conditions, he holds the option of declining the honour in the last hour.

Those readers who can identify themselves as right-arm personalities will agree they are indeed a cheery lot; whatever their group — a professional society, ladies' auxiliary, or masonic lodge — they, least of all, have cause to tremble when the rumblings through the group grapevine signal the discontent of underlings for the overlords. As the complaints of aloofness and snobbery begin to filter through to the listening ears, the right-arm of the chief of the ladies' auxiliary can well afford her complacent smile. She has status without danger. She enjoys life in the group. She has the best of two worlds: she is right in with the top lady who desperately needs her and she's in with all the carpers below who still tolerate the 'likeable right-arm'.

Making up the majority of the membership in any group of one's early adulthood are, of course, those individuals who settle, at least temporarily, for a niche in society that is one rung further down on the political ladder; one could label such status a 'left-arm' position. In political circles these are the party workers; in other group situations their counterparts include, for example, the cheer leaders at sporting events; the canvassers and the pollsters and those out soliciting for various worthy social causes all reflect other aspects of the intermediary station in the hierarchy of group structure. The psychological motivations of these left-arms appear on the surface simple to evaluate; most obviously operating are those human strivings that lift a young person into the altruism so typical of the adolescent period of life, something that allows him to enrol in the service of a cause. Without young zealots to share the workload and to do the footwork, leaders and their executive would be paralysed. But apart from their being 'called', one cannot ignore certain other dynamisms which by no means point either to altruistic or to philanthropic motivations.

Many workers, relegated as they are to the most menial and degrading of stations within the structure of a group, naturally harbour an ambition to emerge from their own shroud of anonymity and to attract public notice. Most of us become imbued with a yearning sometime in our adolescence to become a 'somebody', to be more than just another face in the crowd. The matter of translating these ambitions into actuality is a phenomenon that in some instances carries the driving force of pure instinctual aggression. Robert Lane (1959) perceives the arena of politics as a prime modality for the relief of human aggressive tension; for example he most properly pinpoints the unconscious reactionary aggressions of many leftists who attempt to conceal their hostilities with an ideology of the brotherhood of man and who never quite succeed in transcending these same aggressions. Lasswell's earlier treatise (1930) on political agitators highlights the instinctual component in those who use politics as a means of solving a disturbed personal life. To my mind, this work suffers from an overemphasis on individual psychopathology in explaining group processes; the homage to psychiatry is overdone, which is understandable considering that Lasswell was one of the first of those political scientists to embrace Freudian concepts of individual psychology as having relevance to politics.

Perhaps we can better understand those forces (excluding ideological passions) that cause us to externalize our ambitions in public political participation by looking beyond either the instincts of raw aggression or pure libido to explain these forces. I would suggest that the agitation toward externalizing one's ambitions in the field of politics is consciously motivated in many instances by the hunger for some acknowledgment from those around us. The clash between strivings for recognition by an outside world, and fears of being found unacceptable by that same world, is expressed in the compromise symptom of exhibitionism.

The tendency toward exhibitionism begins, of course, in our earliest years and is by no means peculiar to neurotics or to societal leaders. It is an affliction shared by that segment of humanity which, to all purposes, tends to remain submerged within the anonymity of the group. There are limitless examples of bizarre public performances, some bordering on the pathological, that certain people demonstrate in their craving to be a 'somebody'. What may appear in childhood to be simply a tendency toward sexual curiosity and explorativeness — a predilection in a youngster to display what he considers his most esoteric and charismatic parts — often in fact reflects a more fundamental desire simply to be noticed. An intensification of this need can frequently lead to defiant exhibitionistic transgressions. The young sexual 'offender', for example, who leaps from the bushes with his genitals exposed for their shock effect on the prim lady next door, may not only be expressing a childish delight in such indiscreet behaviour, but in his exhibitionism he may be testing society for its acknowledgment of what for him may be 'dubious wares'.

The same sort of conflict is translated during one's school years into more intellectual and academic pursuits; instead of showing our private parts in public, we begin to modify our earlier 'ego trips' by performances in 'show and tell' and other devices aimed at finding our niche. Yet even from such innocent exhibitionistic displays, there emerges in many young students a host of psychological symptoms that brings them to the offices of school psychologists – professional workers whose lot it is to deal primarily with those school phobias and stage frights that often relate to the child's first efforts in public oratory. Patients in psychiatric consultation bring vivid recollections of these childhood fears, among them the fear of defecating in their pants during the 'show and tell' of their school days. It is exhibitionism that drives some females to satisfy their craving by a striptease or that compels the comedian to act up both on and off the stage. Many professional comics see themselves as the victims of some diabolical force that drives them to externalize in a manner they themselves find offensive; as one professional entertainer put it, 'I'm tired of exposing my pornography to rabble who have me at their mercy!' But his insight in no way could appease his compulsion to practise what for him was a distastefully exhibitionistic profession.

The world of politics is a prime area that lends itself to exhibitionism, whether one is a left arm or a right buttock within the anatomical structure of the group. In the minds of many a worker lurks the secret hope that by hovering around the top people he may be chosen for a more starring role. How many young women at party headquarters during that last election have not wished to become 'the one and only' when it comes to fetching the candidate's coffee after a long night of campaigning! Like the girls in the back line of the chorus, they too are looking to be 'discovered'. In politics, one is legitimized by one's involvement in the now socially syntonic discharge of one's exhibitionism; here is a perfect vehicle for the individual to show himself off. And in these times more than ever, politics lifts our exhibitionism to the glamourous level of the activist. No more are we merely children jumping from bushes when we parade *en masse* with our placards on high: the fact that much of our activist posture is derived from early forbidden impulses that relate to the exposure of our private parts is of little consequence in the public world of politics. What would have passed in our childhood as a perversion now becomes the mark of a patriot.

I am not saying that political demonstrations are simply the expression of sexual perversion, any more than I am criticizing them as fraudulent displays passing as ideological expression. Brought to an externalized level by a youth fiercely engaged in the affairs of their country, ideological activism is a bulwark of democracy. None the less, the vehicle of politics does allow a permeation and an enmeshment of the unsolved exhibitionistic tendencies of men and women, and some people do find an expedient outlet in such self-inflationary performances; they are no longer considered exhibitionists, but activists.

The clash of ideologies is never more demonstrable than it is in the exhibitionistic displays of the adolescent as he confuses a political ideology with a niche in a society that values fame or notoriety. In such a paradox, the adolescent demonstrates against violence by acts of violence; he repudiates the double standard of the system by exerting the most strenuous efforts to qualify for some special niche in that very system; he demands a classless society in which his particular exhibitionism lifts him out of the classless; his communal slogan is 'to let it all hang out', yet he is determined to let 'his' hang out just a little bit further than his fellows.

In their quest for their particular niche in politics, young adults are far from being willing to settle as some unimportant appendage in the political body that involves them. Like other members of my profession, I have had ample opportunity to follow many an adolescent who has shown a preoccupation with trying for a charisma of his own. I feel it is not unkind to describe some of these people as hoaxters. One young man stands out especially in my mind because he so aptly illustrates man's quest for a niche as well as the fine line that exists sometimes between hoax and reality. 'Duke' was a sophomore at university, planning to major in sociology and to go on to politics or law, when he first came to me for some help. Fathered by a man who had worked his way up to become a reasonably successful chiropodist, Duke's political interests were unconsciously related to defeating this 'apparition' of a father who prowled about the house like an ape wearing nothing but a hernia truss. This parent was the constant target for the shrill invective of the 'woman' by the kitchen sink who endlessly eviscerated what to Duke always seemed the same scrawny chicken. It was the attempt to fill his father's shoes in living up to the ambitions of a cavernously engulfing mother that gave Duke's personality from his earliest years a definite aura of hoax; he spent a long adolescence posturing as something that he wasn't.

Extremely involved in campus politics, Duke managed to make loud and threatening noises as an activist, outdoing his colleagues to a point where he felt destined to make it to the very top as a charismatic leader on campus. As he described it, his glamour faded on the dismal day when he became unmasked. All too painfully, he related the vivid moment when he failed his crucial test. The situation pleaded for some kind of heroics amid a special group confrontation between the president of the university and campus revolutionaries: someone had to rise from the audience, stomp majestically to the podium where the 'great man' stood at the microphone, and forcibly wrest the communication system from the establishment's very hands. The rest can be anticipated. First came Duke's queasy stomach, then the exaggerated mental images, the fantasied struggle between revolutionary son and some vague ape, a trembling of limbs, a mouth run dry. All Duke's ambitions for a personal charisma went down the drain that day! It was left, in fact, to one of his more robust comrades to do the job.

I have had a letter or two from Duke since those years of his big splash on campus. He is now a junior in a legal firm and tells me that he is now finding expression for his charismatic polemics through the processes of law.

THE SEXUAL NICHE

Politics is not the only major vehicle for finding a niche in society. The area of human sexuality has today become as well something of an arena for 'ego trips'. Far from being simply an expression of an instinctual sexual passion or of a show of love or a wish to procreate the species, it is instead for many a vehicle in the quest for an ego identity and a niche in society. So-called feminist or women's liberation movements, to which belong a swelling number of the younger male population, do not yet have a standard package of demands for women's 'liberation'.

In these times women have been taking increasingly strenuous issue about the status of the female in society. Today some women are fully convinced that they have no more obligation for maternal care to their offspring than do the fathers of their children; even the nursing of their infants is perceived by many as an antiquated bovine activity from which women should be liberated or, in a world of synthetic foods, which should be equally shared by the male. To such women, the mammary glands are totally disowned as organs of nutriment. At the material end of the pole, there are many feminists who not only demand equal rights in a social and economic sense but feel that there should be a place for a woman to be out earning the bread and butter while the man stays home to play mother.

One can well sympathize with those who actively agitate for changes in the stereotyped role traditionally attached to the female in our society — basically a second-class status of concubinage. One can concede the logic of those who can no longer tolerate the demeaning of the female sex by commercials exploiting the female image. One can agree that society should dispense with the caricature image from old British movies in which, as the classic symbol of gracious feminine charm, an arthritic little old lady sits in a wheelchair, castrated of all her moving parts. One can also agree with the logical rights of women to have state-supplied nurseries for those who must make a livelihood. Furthermore, the rights of women to decide what they do with their own biological procreativity relative to both conception and abortion is long overdue.

For the more militantly inclined members of women's liberation, where nothing short of an equivalent regime of life for both sexes is acceptable, there is cause, however, for qualms and even alarm. Philosophically logical though such an idea may appear, it falls apart when one recognizes that many such militants have confused liberation from societal oppressions that impede the entitlement of females to their sense of wholeness with liberation from social censures that inhibit women from aggressing against the male in a move toward sharing his masculine entitlements. The argument that power is not sex-differentiated is fallacious. The power implicit in material goods, status, and prestige has clearly no gender, but the power of a woman to nurture her young with her breasts, and to love and procreate with her genital apparatus, cannot possibly be shared or made equal to the phallic endeavours of the male. Many of the militant liberationists that I have encountered have shown an unawareness about how many aggressors there really are in their so called struggle for liberation. They claim (and rightfully) that the rivalrous male holds them back from gaining power: yet in these very liberationists there often lurks an unconscious expectation of sharing the power of the male rather than developing their own power.

To those in the field of psychology, it is apparent that today's young adult has a new problem. Rather than simply suffering in large measure, as he always has, from sexual conflicts to do with instinctual inhibitions vis-à-vis the proprieties and ethics of family and community, he is plagued instead by a rather alarming character disturbance — a disturbance in sexual identity. Directly related to this disturbance is the appearance of new chemicals, including the contraceptive pill as well as various stimulant drugs associated very closely with sexual expression. There is no question that the pill has allowed modern-day woman an opportunity for a niche in society that she could not have attained without it. A chemical designed for the enlightened society, the pill, along with abortions and sterilizations, has given a impetus to the new ideology of youth, energized not only by the realistic dangers of world destruction, pollution, of over-population, but by their need for causes and for finding a niche in society.

Like all innovative elements that have marked the progress of a society — a progress that itself relates to doing away with some of the hazards of ill health, of overpopulation, of poverty, and of global pollution — the use and abuse of the pill have provoked psychological complications. Sex has long been harnessed by mechanical contraceptive interventions, to prevent the dangers to health and the problems of economic security that result from unwanted conceptions. Although these interventions have been for the welfare of mankind, none the less, in one way or another, they did not serve to deform man's hunger for healthy sexual expression or com-promise his natural bent toward the procreation of his species. The psychic identities of the man and the woman in a sexual union was, in the main, preserved.

Now comes the pill, and mankind's stronghold for a psychological sense of identity has been invaded by synthetic hormones, which along with yet newer hormones for the male (still in the testing stage) abort the basic biological functions of the human body. This is psychologically equi-valent to hormonal plastic surgery on the vital organs of the individual who uses this chemical. The same invasion of both anatomical and psychic identity occurs increasingly frequent-ly in sterilization surgery of one kind or another. The pre-servation of health and life justifies such emergency mea-sures in many instances: but surgery performed through the collusion of neurotic patient and doctor often invites psychological repercussions of an irrevocable order. Anyone who suggests that a sexual act between a man and a woman does not become altered psychologically by the use of an artificial device, whether chemical, surgical, or mechanical, is hopelessly misinformed.

For the adolescent of a by-gone era, the sex act represented a fearsome risk; it was through the agonizing work of a developing ago that the youngster learned to neutralize his sex impulses, to subdue the storms of natural lust, and to sublimate instinct as part of the creativeness of a civilized being. As his body grew taller and his impulses stronger, the adolescent had to learn, unsuccessfully at times, that responsibilities went along with the need to love; his instincts became bent with all the inventive plasticity that the human mind could mobilize. Desperately, the adolescent clung to a philosophy that would preserve nature — even as he watched his elders of the establishment wage war against their fellow men and pollute their own land with their 'advances' in urbanization and industrialization. Now comes youth's ecological revolution: 'preserve plant, animal and human life at all costs' is the cry of the new ecology. So, on a bandwagon dedicated to the primacy of nature, there comes a package of chemical magic pushed the world over by the hormone-mongers. In a huge paradox, youth's key equipment for this new naturalist society is pills, drugs, and sexual surgery!

The sexual niche in society sought for by so many of our young men today seems to be little more than mechanical laboratory experimentation. As of now, it is easy to find a girl on the pill; she is 'turned on': her youthful mate in many instances is equally 'turned off'. His easily available 'target practice' proves he is a man of the world and offers him a niche on his belt as well as in his society. But at times he is so sexually alienated that he finds 'making love to the pill' like fornicating with an effigy or a knothole in a fence.

To the teenage girl, the rights of her elders to use hormones and sometimes surgery for the protection of health and the necessary limitations of family escape her. She is still at the stage where she demands a single standard for elders and youth alike, and she cannot quite fathom why her mother would be willing to use a pill that might jeopardize her own health and maybe her own life by disrupting a menarche for the family good, yet at the same time violently deplore this disruption in the young body of a daughter. Pubertal girls whose physiological cycle has hardly been solidly established are already placing themselves in jeopardy by the impulse to conform to a growing society of 'pharmacy girls'.

With the invasion of natural hormonal functioning and its associated passions by a synthetic world of mechanics and chemicals, there comes a stagnating sexual indifference, an apathy, and a boredom with it all. But to the rescue comes a new sexology! Sexual scientists record the pulsations of the human libido in action on sound track, on wide screen, and in full colour. 'We'll wire you for grunt, groan, and thrust, and give you a reading on the libido meter!' Here is the ultimate in Pavlovian coitus, the latest in 'ego trips', a new selective mating completely unrelated to the love of man for woman or woman for man.

A search for an ego identity in this engineered sexuality is doomed; it can only promote a character pathology where formerly there was a problem of sexual inhibition. Even animals cannot get away with such artificially staged solutions; there are well-documented psychological experiments (Harlow 1959, 1962) carried out under laboratory conditions where it was demonstrated that monkeys could be taught to accept nourishment — a kind of make-shift maternal sustenance — from mechanical robot monkeys and still manage to survive. But there were certain complications that such artificially sustained monkeys invariably demonstrated in their subsequent behaviour; they developed profound disturbances in their personalities and in their social and sexual behaviour; they showed bizarre patterns of aggressive responses — indeed confusion in their sense of identity.

With human beings it is not far-fetched to predict that the so-called sexual revolution could follow a course where not only will the male's sexual functions be placed in serious jeopardy of extinction, but the female procreative functions will be profoundly affected as well, a direct consequence of the intricate relationship between the two sexes. Even as matters stand now, psychologists' offices are becoming populated with more and more females suffering from the 'goldfish syndrome' — psychologically infertile women spending hours gazing at the goldfish tanks in the waiting rooms of their gynecologists. Motivated ostensibly toward the promotion of fertility, many such women are unwittingly ambivalent about conception through their own unconscious rebellion against it or through the often secret, yet valid, mistrust they harbour for their already undermined and irresponsible male partners.

THE CULTURAL NICHE

The hunger for a niche in society is not peculiar to youth alone; it accounts for many of the foibles in the behaviour of humans of all ages. The efforts of an individual to find a place in the sun has often led him to compulsions to acquire an identity by association that at times have teetered on the ridiculous. I hold the individual suspect who denies ever having rubbed shoulders at one time or another with someone he regards as an elevating influence toward his own cultural ambitions. One's hunt for such a niche in more artistic society is most manifest in the climactic period of one's life, when problems of self-esteem and old adolescent qualms about achieving one's ideals become reactivated. Perhaps the older reader will more easily identify himself in this category of 'culture vulture'. It is always amazing to take stock of the amount of energy we expend groping for just a little bit of the aesthetic world.

For example, take the formal opening of a new arts centre or gallery. There is a rather stereotyped procedure. Arriving upon the scene, you find people like yourself already queued up in large herds, like unsuspecting cattle outside an abattoir. Inside the gallery, you stretch and crane as the dignitaries make their grand advance — the curator, the mayor, and so on, all in their full plumage. First come the croakings of the curator as he unfolds the saga of the city's cultural achievements down through the years. Then perhaps a sculpture is unveiled; the artist receives a standing ovation; and the event goes on to its logical conclusion as the audience comes forward to inspect from close range — not the work of art but the artist himself.

At the reception that follows, everyone fawns over the artist, and the entourage of politicians, of course, attempts to be equally noticed. And every hanger-on, yourself included, imputes his own unworthy motives to his fellow travellers in this orgy of identity by association. You look about for a fellow ignoramus in this artistic conclave, and immediately discover all your counterparts shifting back and forth from one sandwich platter to another, gobbling everything in sight with a desperate compulsion. Edgingly you brush against the man of the hour, the 'master' himself, prattling just a little and dimly aware that the nonsense that comes from your lips represents some alien force that you never conceived as belonging to you. Heady on your fourth sherry, your cheeks bulging with olives, sea-foods, and other less identifiable objects, you fumble for the check to your coat. And later, while driving home through the slush and snowy drizzle, you know that when it comes to art, you are no more 'with it' on departure than you were when you arrived. Yet you suspect that, on receiving your next engraved invitation to a similar soirée, you will go back for more.

Most of us then, but some of us sooner than others, come to a point of accepting the idea of a communal hero or heroine other than ourselves occupying the topmost niche in our society. For ourselves, we manage to find a token success in our social endeavours, we manage a few sexual 'ego trips', and culturally we rub shoulders with an artist or two. We may have experienced the tug of a calling that afforded us a left-arm status in some local politics and, at the national level, we may have written a letter to a major newspaper. Though it all adds up to something less than the niche that we had earlier thought would be ours, we can compensate for this by climbing on the bandwagon of a 'hero', projecting onto him our covert, albeit frustrated, desire to fight for the biggest role and the charismatic niche of the national leader.

Chapter 6

The big fight

Biological survival depends on procreation and propagation, and this is true also for the continuance of charismatic imagery. Let us now examine the media that circulate and disseminate the images that our unique and individual imaging processes feed on.

The medium today with the greatest effect on the charismatic process is, of course, television, and the simplest approach to political image-making is to follow what television offers in the field of sales and commerce. It is our own imagery, carefully researched by professionals, that is eventually played back in 'the commercial'. The tapping of the subconscious in human behaviour is so skilfully accomplished here that the whole process appears to follow a simple formula: yet advertising has become intricately and sophisticatedly geared to impinge on that particular stratum of the public psyche that regulates its buying. It is impressive how successful the blatantly obvious techniques in marketing are.

A new brand of bubbly drink is 'pitched' to the public in the same fashion as a politican is frothed up for office; both presentations are intended to bring out the romantic flavour of the product. In this swinging pitch, the soft-drink consumer is made to believe that the image of this new bottle of elixir is so much a basic part of his heroic and freedom-loving identity that he had better get some before the supply runs out. A similar equation holds between the promotion of certain mellow ales and an establishment-type political image; both represent stability and tradition. The bottled fluid is displayed to the public as a well-matured vital juice — a traditional security for our everyday lives; the buyer is warned that without such a vintaged lifeline from such an old reliable establishment he might well, in the uncertain future, be left a weak and helpless thing: 'I give you (roll of drums) brew from the house of Krutz', vibrates the majestic voice of a tankard-clutching salesman from his easy-chair by a (dummy) hearth.

The more coercive impact of the traditional image contrasts with the seductive invitation of the new elixir — a distinction similar to that between the coercive posture of Freud's 'great man' and the seduction typical of charismatic imagery. The dramatists who symbolize tradition and the people's communal conscience rely especially on sound to transmit their death-knell message to anyone contemplating a crime against the state: an unbelievably bass voice will boom out the ten transgressions for which the victim of the show has been indicted on all counts.

All this is in stark contrast to the seductive image: here we have a much more libido-oriented invitation that baits us to indulge in all the sensual elements that could possibly exist between a child and its mother or a man and his mistress or wife. Seductive imagery carries an aura of liberalism, holding a promise of breaking down all parochial barriers usually associated with a more traditional imagery. Yet such liberalism is achieved by the delicate use of a reverse psychology: the product is set up as seemingly exclusive, for it appeals not only to the particular class seductively honoured but is also shrewdly designed to draw in as well all those so suggestively excluded. This results, of course, in the widest and most indiscriminate circulation of the product — in fact to every class of both the gullible and the addictive. The cigarette made only 'for the girl who is emancipated' swiftly ends up in the mouth of a truck-driver.

The field of merchandising has a much broader scope for sexual imagery than does the field of politics, since merchandising carries no sex taboo and can make all possible use of libido. Politicians never introduce direct references to sexuality in their manipulation of public opinion, for an open attack on a political opponent that related to his sexuality in any way could boomerang and fragment the solidarity of the attacking group. It could promote individualized sexual reactions, always a sure disrupting influence on the psychological dynamics of any group. Image-makers for political figures must often regret that they cannot use libido in the flagrant way a professional promotes and markets a new tonic water. For the latter, no risk is run at all; it is an

advantage to sales if the consumer develops a personal instinctual relationship with his soft drink and its streamlined
bottle; full-scale sexualized seduction offers an extra spice to
living, a respite from the treadmill of his drab life, his choice
of beautiful girls who handle each bottle on television with a
gentle stroking caress. In politics this overt sexuality cannot
possibly be duplicated, since it is dangerous to group
cohesion and certainly incongruous with charismatic sexuality as it applies to public figures. There would be chaos if
politicians used the same sexual plays as bottle mongers on
·television.

But in selling charisma in politics, a little pinch of libido —
just enough to whet the appetite — can be sneaked in as a
blend of play and good humour. The professional handlers
and promoters — anarchistic agents, I remind you — do their
job well, shrewdly guessing that you and I are just about
ready to be 'turned on'. Anyone yearning for a change of
pace looks for the nectar pressed from a 'leaf from the vine
of Eros'. But the image must not be too blatant: there is no
direct reference to sexual ambitions, no singling out of any
favourites in the egalitarian society; rather, just some hints of
erotic play, just some delicate aura of hanky-panky. There
lurks a wish in everyone for an endless repetition of the
pleasure principle; and every voting citizen has to be allowed
that tug to the earliest origins of group structure, to the very
beginnings of culture, to the meaningful and erotic tie to his
mother.

With our projections primed to achieve a respite from the
burdens of reality, we look to our professional image-maker
to offer a leader whose image captures the premise of an old
familiar liberation from structured environmental forces; in
play we will find our independence supreme! Surely we
should not be denied at least one contestant in the 'big fight'
who can capture the combined elements of play and sexuality, and become an image out of mythology — a symbol of
Eros revisited. Through the magic of television, we look for
an image who can conduct us through a symphonic exercise

in surplus erotic energy not required in the task of survival, a figure that reminds us that culture is a product of man's leisure rather than of the sweat of his brow. In his infectious playfulness, he will transmit the message that we too can construct, in our own play, a world transformed in accord with our own image, that we too can emancipate ourselves from the exigencies of daily life and utilize our energies so conserved toward those sophisticated elements of living that give content to our own personal charisma.

Let us all not be too coarse in our playfulness, however. As in creative artistry, there is no room for crudeness, no call for an exposure of the origins of the playful elements involved. Like artists of sorts, both we and our leader must learn to disguise these roots so as to direct our activities toward a participation in aesthetic illusion. As in the make-believe of children, we must ensure that neither player nor audience deviates from this formula: if either treats the make-believe as legitimately real or as complete fantasy, then the illusion will be destroyed. We must preserve the fibre of illusion and weave it into the fabric of our charismatic mannikin.

The whole world loves a lover; and in the televised display of national politics the whole world loves a playboy. We all receive a television treat — 'playboy under glass'! Our charismatic contestant on camera should be smiling; the electorate can no more accept the puckered brow of care on the face of its charismatic leader than children can accept the clouded mien of a disenchanting parent. The deepest and most primal security in leadership lies in the perception of our man at play. How comforting for all of us during a time of crisis to observe our tanned man of state waterskiing over the rippling blue of some scenic lake or enjoying a leisurely round of golf as serene testimony to the illusion that all is under control. And when night begins to fall, we want our man decked out in black tie and boutonnière, dancing on the plaza roof, a glamour queen enfolded in his embrace, cha-cha-cha! But we want our man out of bed bright and early the next morning, back in the House, baggy eyes and all, settling affairs of state with immaculate precision.

And let us have a sense of humour about the whole thing! Let our leader tell for us a few jokes at the right moment. After all, elements of a people's mirth include the same in-gredient of familiarity as do the other elements of charisma. The joke is a playful judgment and as such is connected with freedom, binding into a unity ideas that are basically alien to one another. Jokes bring out something concealed or hidden and they have a charm that causes one person to transmit them to another. In the service of rebellion against authority, the caricature of those whom we regard as too powerful for our comfort offers us a comical relief from such oppression. The most important relationship of jokes to charisma is the perpetuation of illusion, where truth is both hidden and ex-posed, especially the truth of one's basic and familiar defec-tiveness, one's imperfection. The leader who jokes saves us all energy; there is economy in humour. The topicality of a new joke offers us a freshness and an illusion of virginity; though the core of the joke carries an old familiar ring and contains the basic spice of the humour, the application of the joke to current events gives it a novel outer coating that yields us a bonus in pleasure. As with other charismatic phenomena, we react in particular to whatever in the joke plays us the subtle deficiencies that burden humanity in their struggle with the images of an overpowering external world.

THE PRELIMINARIES

In politics, as in any big fight for the championship of the world, a tournament must be drawn up and all the hopefuls are expected to participate in an elimination series. In demo-cratic societies, unlike countries behind the Iron Curtain, such a tournament is an open affair where the people (as well as the contestants) participate in one form or another, and more directly, of course, in the finals. But up to these last phases of the battle, their participation is far less noticeable. Everyone is well aware that the system of party delegates who decide these vital elimination issues still leaves much to be desired for a properly run election; the in-fighting, the backroom lobbying, the intrigues, and the block-voting cliques — these have enjoyed far too long a heyday in any proper representational system.

Granted we need reforms, but nevertheless we the people are by no means completely out of the picture at these elimination trials. Each of us carries his own package of psychic imagery which, from the very embryonic stages of its conception, has become moulded and modified with growth and experience into ideals and ideologies — the emblematic colours of which cry out for some champion or knight in shining armour. Our inventive imagery becomes projected onto the political structure of our times in the form of a kaleidoscopy of gladiators who have pledged themselves to carry the banners, the colours, and the symbols of our varied idealizations. One of the most hopeful elements in our democracy is that just about every colour within the spectrum of human ideals is worn by one knight or other in the elimination jousts.

The script of these elimination trials unfolds in the same dramatic sequence as the Queen's Plate, the Belmont stakes, or the Derby. Despite the declaration of the expected entries, there is always that stir of uncertainty and excitement drummed up by all the racing touts (anarchists), both on and off the track, looking to promote some last-minute speculation. Augmenting this aura of enigma are the cryptic pronouncements of both owner and trainer of Charisma, the horse considered by most to be the fastest in the field. The message right up to trumpet call is predictably unpredictable: 'maybe Charisma will go to the post — and then again maybe he won't!' Naturally the people in the stands are buzzing with expectancy; they have not come out just for the fresh air or merely to place their bets; they are not there to fritter away their time with a 'win, place, or show' on a herd of Clydesdales while the best colt to come out of Foreign Dancer chomps on his oats back in Hyannisport. They are at the track to see their gleaming thoroughbred Charisma out on the turf with his favourite jockey (image-maker). Paradoxical as it may seem, the electorate are like racing fans; they do stand procrastination from their heroes; they tolerate some waiting — a dry-run to test a game leg, for example. They will even permit Charisma one last-minute scratch, provided he makes ready for a come-from-behind win at the wire in the final stakes.

Before we move to the finals, we must ensure the nomination of a 'great man' to run against the charismatic hero in the 'big fight'. We must have a 'Mister Establishment'. Let him have sombreness, a furrowed brow, lots of self-discipline, an image of law and order, and lots of 'ponder'. Let us have a quiet man, long accustomed to breathing unpolluted air, but also a man of action who can yet withdraw to the seat of the thinker for noble soliloquy or contact with the divinity. We ask for very little from this man: we want the familiar coercive patriarch, a diligent hard-working, responsible citizen, yet opulent and powerful.

This is the archetypal line-up: 'ponder' in the one corner, and 'cool charisma' in the other. Television enhances this polarity, but it is a little different — a little disconcerting in fact — closer to the actual process. Take the business of a legislature for example, where the proceedings can in some instances be likened to the protocol of the 'outhouse gang' of one's boyhood years. I remember one visit to the Ontario Legislature at which the antics of the provincial representatives came across as one big 'caper'. For sure, there are always a few disturbers in any house of representatives, people acting up for self-amusement or for public notoriety; but it is an awakening experience to witness our governors in the hall of authority sprawled on their backsides reading the newspaper, occasionally tearing themselves from the sports section to heckle, to hurl invective, or to thump their desks in gestures of alertness. Some frustrated backbencher is delivering an endless barrage of nonsense, a deliberate filibuster to prevent anything from being achieved. The pageboys keep flitting back and forth from one snoring member to another, appearing to deliver important messages by tray, yet clearly performing their basic function of awakening those who have succumbed to boredom. You find yourself making a mental note that, if you ever became chief, you would have television infiltrate every corner of every house of legislation in the country; then there would be some changes when the 'gang' realized they were all candidly on camera.

A national convention viewed from an armchair at home on television is different. It has some disturbing features, yet you are thankful to live in an age when you can witness all this pageantry — about one hour of business and five hours of carnival. Shirtless and with a bottle of Krutz by your side, you wait impatiently for the action. A touch of drama at last: the chairman, perspiring in telegenic blue, pounds his gavel in hopeless efforts at controlling the random movements of delegates, a mob whose deportment seems about as responsible as a moosehunters' guild on their weekly bowling night. Still, there is some intrigue as the party politicians begin bending the will of the popcorn-happy delegates from the hinterlands. But not all that goes on is openly exposed to the public, for the role of the commentators, like that of the chorus in a Greek play, is to 'cover' and patch over the political intrigue to maintain an aura of dignity to the play. Their 'in-talk' on such matters as the 'erosion of upstate support' and the 'seepage of voting strength' may make us wonder, as one newsman put it, 'if we're watching a sales convention for septic tanks!' Naturally, the electronic age also brings some new dramatic forms, such as the eventual presentation of the election results. And there is a computer, a brand-named 'character' who prophesies the outcome, like a modern Tiresias.

But in all the carnival of convention time and the fever of election day, one thing does become clear to everyone, namely that it is the people, you and I, who hold the trump card — our own private ballot. You and I become the final referee in the 'big fight'; you and I bring in the verdict! We shuffle the imprints from our developmental imagery and deal ourselves a handful of aces and kings; we have held our rehearsals, projected our ideological themes, manipulated our players and had them read the lines of the script that we, *en masse,* have selected as the play of the year. As promoters, directors, producers, choreographers, and composers, we have set down the music, the lyrics, and the action to our own creative artistry, in the fashioning of a charismatic leader in our own image. Soon we shall mark our x on a piece of paper — and that will be it: the final verdict!

The script of the political passion play, as written by the people, calls for two leading characters, villain and hero. Many of us who enjoy that extra suspense leave the matter of who is to play whom until the last minute; there are those who have even admitted to changing their minds right in the polling booth. Some even select the one who is to play hero *after* the election; for these people, it is the one who actually receives the mandate that counts: the loser becomes automatically villain, strangely enough. To others still, it is the other way round — the winner becomes the villain and the loser the hero; in this bracket fall those people who can only empathize with the underdog. Many, of course, do not vote at all, and the naive assumption is that they have no interest. Not so! Many who fail to show at the polls are expressing a vote in absentia — these are one segment of the anarchists I spoke of before.

THE RESPONSIBLE VOTER

The driving force in our electoral system that generates and allocates power is an organized structure, the polity, whose functions, as contrasted with those of government, are to build the necessary framework that affords the latter its opportunity to assume and discharge its responsibilities. Standing at the controls of political organizations are the party officials, and the fulcrum of the mechanization that implements government in a democratic society is the party system. The one process in which the people as a whole have a share in the support of such government, is the casting of their electoral ballot, in so far as voting is the decisive factor in the choosing of leadership. Each member of the group holds both a real as well as a symbolic participatory tie in relationship to his fellow members and to the group's ultimate leader, and these relations are expressed in the reality of his vote.

Social scientists such as Parsons (1967) and Berelson, Lazarsfeld, and McPhee (1954) recognize two kinds of voter, the collective and the individual; in the collective category, they place persons who tend to vote *en bloc,* such as union members whose voting reflects their particular class — whether economic, ethnic, ideological, religious, or other. Parsons sees the collective voter as exerting a profound influence in stabilizing society; in contrast, the individual voter, being more prone to individualism, is more sensitive to the personalities involved rather than to the politics of the leadership. Such voters he labelled independents — people who create a flexibility, a shifting of political allegiances, a tendency toward instability; such individuals upset traditional patterns by influencing politics in directions that are, in one way or another, in opposition to the ideologies of major parties. Parsons feels that these independents are by no means well informed in politics, are not very interested in the issues of the campaign, but are more bound to inherited patterns and as such, more likely to vote with those who share their much more individualized ideology; they are less interested in for what they vote than for whom they vote. He contrasts them to the group voters, who are, by and large, influenced by the conscious issues of traditionalism; individual voters are more under the sway of unconscious forces in choosing their candidate or leader. Parsons sees political multi-party systems as mechanisms that operate to afford a relative equilibrium in our pluralistic society, wherein maverick groups of one kind of another are continually shifting allegiances between traditional modes of political life at one end, and breakthrough politics at the other end, of the spectrum. He feels that a highly personalized and unconsciously driven individualist is pitted against the traditionalism of the collective order (Progressive Conservatives and Liberals; Republicans and Democrats; Conservatives and Labour), thus bringing about a stable degree of neutralization of these two traditional polarities. Parsons' model, of course, is most applicable to the politics of the United States, whose 'mavericks and independents' could hardly be equated with the New Democratic Party, Social Credit, or the Communists in Canada, where there is increasing evidence of the same collective voting for these particular parties as there is for our more traditional parties.

To a degree, I can concur with Parsons' sociological theory, allowing for the differences in party politics between countries. However, from a more psychologically oriented position, one would have to classify things somewhat differently. I would identify two kinds of voter, but argue that both types are significantly influenced by unconscious processes. In my terms, I have to think of voting citizens as either responsible or irresponsible, according to the degree of maturity with which they cast their ballot. Responsible voters may be either independents or party members, but they are individuals who cast their ballot for a leadership whose ideology and whose individual and communal conscience most closely approximates the ideology they hold themselves. The actual leader then represents a proxy or a stand-in for a voting citizen who, in his vote, takes his full burden of responsibility for the nation's governmental apparatus and for the conscience expressed in these politics.

By contrast, the irresponsible voter is one who psychologically abdicates his full adult responsibility. He too may vote either collectively as a party member or as an independent, but in either case he is liable to surrender the formulation of a full adult ideology or communal conscience to the mentality of the leader, who thus in effect becomes such a citizen's conscience. This abdicating citizen takes little responsibility for government; often he may abstain from voting; if he does cast a ballot, it is commonly in a mechanical exercise of his franchise or motivated perhaps by some uniquely private interests. Democracy does not capture a sense of the full sharing of responsibility in such a citizen. Perhaps the most pertinent feature in the psychology of such an individual's vote is his expression of all those infantile and adolescent romantic residues that he has been unwilling to outgrow in the search for more adult responsibilities to himself and to others.

I differ then from Parsons as to just which voters are under the sway of their unconscious. Certain people continue in their so-called adult lives in directions still heavily under the influence of adolescent and infantile forces which they have not only failed to outgrow but of which they are not fully aware. An adolescent, though to an extent retaining the uniqueness of a conscience derived primarily from his private family romance, becomes increasingly aware as he moves further into the group situation, of both his individual limitations of personality as well as his need for a corroboration of his own sense of legitimate individuality; because of his qualms of ineffectuality, he commonly undergoes varying degrees of altruistic surrender to the camaraderie of a group identification. This surrender links him with others, either in a common bond of inferiority and homage to some patriarchal or matriarchal leader, or in a common bond of revolutionary reaction against such leading figures. What is happening to him is that his ideals are undergoing certain modifications, undergoing a blending and an interpenetration of his own family romance with both the personal fantasies of others as well as the traditional communal myth of his era. This whole process accounts for the establishment of two qualitatively different versions of an immature group ideology. These two together I label the *collective family romance*.

The first version of this romantic group idealization embraces a parental figure, the adopted leader; most commonly this is the 'great man', the patriarch (occasionally it is the primal mother, the matriarch). The second version of the romance brings on stage the heroic revolutionary son or daughter who, by political coup or militant insurrection, overwhelms the patriarch's control over his empire.

To translate these two romantic versions of the people's choice into the realities of politics, one can find ample evidence to indicate that, in most of the large groups in a democratic society, there are always individuals who perceive their ego as rather impotent, leaders outside then being idealized so as to appear gigantic by comparison. Such a state of affairs multiplied many times over within any group makes their particular selection of a leader (out of impotence as it were) not too difficult an undertaking; such a leadership could well be labelled an immature choice in traditional leadership. The leader need only possess the typical qualities most commonly related to the traditional politician; the latter is perceived by the helpless and by the dependent as a human of superior strength, a person of power and prestige. The people afford such a figure a coercive image that goes with this prestige and power. Such a leader then will commonly be met halfway by a stereotyped group reaction that affords him a dominant role in the structure of the group. Even other members of the group who might otherwise have adopted a more critical and discriminating attitude in keeping with a more maturely developed conscience are often swept up as well in this group process of *altruistic surrender* by the infectious suggestibility that goes with it. An analogy in individual psychology is the blend of egoism and altruism that operates in homosexuality, where the psychological prize, the mother, is entrusted to a proxy through whom one vicariously repossesses that prize.

We can think then of this traditional pattern of group idealization as an 'impotents anonymous society', where the chosen leader serves as a substitute for some out-of-reach ideal (the major status of the dominant parent) harboured by the traditionally helpless members of the group. The leader supplies a stronger and bolder ego so that the critical faculties and judgments in affairs of state and community are handed over to his wilful exercise. Putting it another way, each individual citizen in this particular category abdicates or surrenders to the dominancy of the figure of a leader who substitutes for each individual member's conscience. Psychologically speaking, the group conscience is not in this instance a reflection of the group but rather of their leader.

In the revolutionary version of the collective family romance, once again there is sufficient evidence that in every democratic society there are many individuals (especially among the young) who, far from feeling small and impotent, are prone to indulge, consciously or unconsciously, in reactionary omnipotent defences in the service of creating illusions of a rugged independence for themselves. Those who undergo such a process in their personal romance fantasy see themselves as the sons and daughters who must rescue society from the 'great man' (some powerful leader in the community establishment). The romanticism of this revolutionary citizenry has a missionary quality, namely to wrest power from a coercive tyrant, often by valiant revolutionary means in accord with the basically irresponsible omnipotence triggering their heroics. Such revolutionary idealizations, because of the narcissism that promotes them, sooner or later become projected onto an outside heroic figure who represents for the romanticist *all that he wishes to be and feels that he can be himself.* Often such a leader becomes pretender to a throne from which he too would continue to subjugate the masses in his own brand of 'great man' dictatorship. The romantic agitators who support such leaders have a deep contempt for all those who stick with the 'great man' image, nurturing as they do a conviction of their own independence, denying as they do any hunger for power. They would steer their own ship, rarely conscious of the true state of their enmeshment in the process of romantic idealization, a process that binds them in their romance with their leader. Often they are convinced of their own innovative qualities, effervescing with break-through ideologies — and rarely suspect that their revolutionary brainstorms are hackneyed versions of the same irresponsible fantasies that disqualified them as minors from participation in representational government. The gist of this is that heroic or charismatic leadership is by no means distinct and different from the so-called traditional leadership. Both are in fact born from the same matrix of narcissism and the process of idealization; both styles of leadership, dictated as they are by the idealization of an electorate that abdicates its own conscience in deference to a leader, involve the creation of a hero in one form or another. In the case of traditional leadership, this comes through a *surrender from impotence:* in charismatic leadership, it comes through a *surrender from illusory omnipotence.*

If one is to think in such terms, then the social forces that establish a climate propitious for a charismatic figure should not be confused with the deeper psychological issue itself. If the historian or political analyst wants to speculate on the factors initiating public charmistic figures, he cannot ignore this basic psychological factor in a people's politics — namely, that the deeper provocative agent that inspires a surrender of adult representational government to any individual force in leadership is a fear in a people of taking adult responsibility for themselves.

The pertinent proposition here can be formulated in this way: that a sufficient psychological regression in a mass of people under conditions of meaningful loss, whether that loss be real or imagined, invariably leads to an agitated group expectation of rescue by an outside person or persons. Sociological explanations accounting for political shifts in styles of leaderships do not alter the fact that, once regression to the romance of leadership occurs in a people, charisma and the 'great man' both, in one sequence or another, must follow as surely as day follows night.

The emergencies in the social reality that have been held to account for the appearance of charismatic leadership have long been recorded. The fear of economic deprivation, of a world overpopulated, of a global holocaust, of an uprising, or of civil war through the weakening or the loss of a patriarchal leadership (through death or defeat), or perhaps more simply a lethargic tranquillity that has hastened a natural regression — all such fears and indifferences can bring forth a charismatic response from a nation. Somehow, it is the call for a hero to overthrow a 'great man' who has limited the initiatives of his people that appears the most common stimulus for bringing on charismatic leadership. On such soil of stagnation, fear, and rebellion, a collective family romance of a mass of people has its exhilarating and often frenzied reactivation — even in those who have achieved a tenuous emancipation to some state of responsible sobriety.

Having stressed then that regressive group dynamisms are significant in the establishment of both styles of romance leadership, I reiterate that, even in a democratic group situation such as exists in our society today, mass psychology continues at times to play a significant role, especially under conditions of crisis. The irresponsible voter or charismatically disposed citizen who continues to seek a romantic leader demonstrates the survival in himself of some need for a kind of love affair with some chosen object of leadership. Such a phenomenon is visible in a segment of the population at election time — a blind hypnotic love for a leader who replaces to some extent the abdicated will of that citizen. The multiplication of this hypnotic process, especially noticeable in the more regression-prone, creates a following and has even led to a mood in some modern societies that has rightly been labelled a mania. It is still frightening to observe in our democratic culture how the continuing relationship of one individual to his fellow through the common quality of altruistic surrender to a power creates, especially in time of any crisis, a chain reaction of hypnotic surrender which represents a *folie en masse* — a general abdication of critical judgments and an abandonment of self-esteem analogous to what happens psychologically in an orgy.

Let us come back now to the views of Parsons and of Berelson, Lazarsfeld, and McPhee. Their collective category of voter is made up of traditionalists, people whose politics reflect their class, their well-informed position relative to political issues and, by inference, their stable sense of responsibility toward national interests. In contrast, by emphasizing the role of unconscious forces as being just as active in the collective category as they are in the individual type, I am in effect denying the feature of responsibility which these writers have attached to this category of citizen. According to my views, an acknowledgment of the influence of the romantic complexes just outlined throws a very different light on the implications of party affiliations. Conscious ideologies pertaining to class, culture, economics, national policies, foreign and domestic issues only *appear*, I suggest, as the only significant influences in collective party politics: at a deeper level, there is a directional undercurrent of psychic forces relating to one's sense of identity, passions that are infiltrated with the deepest of romantic imagery.

In Canada, for example, the multi-party system derives its respective followings to a meaningful degree from these undercurrents. The right-wing political parties may appear generated by the substance of money, by the strength of big business, and by a rightist ideology that respects the freedom and the potency of private enterprise: I prefer to diagnose an equally meaningful psychic imagery that relates to man's obsession with a patriarchal yoke, a durable harness for some of the infantilities of those who would pay homage to the 'great man'. At the other end of the political spectrum, the left wing indulges itself in a socialism that champions the 'little man' in his quest for an economic equality, for a justice and a freedom from the oppressions of a tyrannical patriarchal system. Yet one must have concern for undercurrents of reaction formation that would overthrow the 'great man' and establish an oligarchy with its own form of oppressions and state-controlled regimentations of private mentality and enterprise. The liberal parties are, in the main, of the belief that they represent a mainstream flexibility of ideologies that satisfactorily reconciles the best of all worlds — a just society for the average man, sprinkled liberally with incentives and rewards for the more enterprising zealots. One diagnoses here the image of a romantically tainted elitism fraught with precocities, charismatic innovations, and politically expedient compromises as motivating elements in this party's platform. Finally in the more terroristic and revolutionary movements, riddled with anarchistic cellular structures and infiltrating so many nations from without as well as from within, the anarchists carry the banner of a secular liberation that cries out for equality for all mankind and promises a global Shangri-La, a new world state, where at last everyone can enjoy freedom from all organized leaderships and tyrannies. In depth, it is an underworld of passion and intrigue, in which dissidents, like leaders, must be repetitively liquidated if not by revolution then by the process of attrition — a relentless erosion of conscience that promises, in exchange, the political mirage of some ultimate osmotic union with a primal mother earth in a blissful nirvana.

It is a testimonial to the success of the democratic process that representatives of each of these political positions, coloured as each is by its derivative undercurrents, not only have a major voice in their nation's affairs, but are capable of coexisting in our society.

THE RESCUE

The matrix of the image of both charismatic and traditional leaders has been explored and both found to be derived from the family romance. What then is the uniqueness of charisma? The answer for me is in the quality of the romanticism that is recaptured.

First of all, in charisma there has to be a *rescue*, a rescue invariably perpetrated by a *stigmatized foreigner.* It is taken for granted here that the chosen hero is well versed in playing the part that the people have created for him. The disciples and the worshippers of the charismatic image demand that their leader be classically seductive in his complement to their own narcissistic illusions. They want the leader's image to say to the people, 'I don't need you but you need me'. This is the essence of subtle seduction: any leader who searches for a people's charisma must neither browbeat nor coerce nor even openly acknowledge any overt ambition for high office.

Especially in the last few critical hours before election time, the charismatic leader is well advised to remain — or appear to remain — well removed from the hubbub. The traditional image of the 'great man' shows a pipesmoking outdoorsman roaming the countryside with his favourite hound; the younger charismatic leader might be playfully tossing a ball around on the beach, relaxed, oblivious to the clamour for his leadership. The most ill-advised effort would be to expose the true picture of his floor-pacing and nail-biting as henchmen feed him the first seven votes just in from Back Patch, Maine, or Joe's Arm, Newfoundland.

At last, the leader is ready to come on stage, a creation of the people, conqueror supreme to a vanquished opponent. He may be the hero that many citizens *wish to be and feel they can be.* He will be a symbol of an oedipal victory one way or the other, either for the revolutionary son (or daughter) or the 'great man'. Either way, he will be one to be admired by women and acclaimed by men; he will be the fulfilment of childhood ambitions, of his own and of his following; he will represent a bridge that unites the present with the past, the male with the female, the good with the bad, and the strong with the weak. If he be the charismatic hero, he will represent to the people the fulfilment of a magnificent illusion — that all of us, like that leader, have found the capacity, the power, and the means to cast off the coercive harness of our forefathers in an ultimately successful reunion with the primal pivotal mother.

The masses, in acclaiming their charismatic leader, will romantically recapture at a collective level the very essence of a symbolic rescue of not only their own self-esteem but that of their leader as well. We, the charisma-worshippers, will have expressed our omnipotent convictions that our hero has the same need to be rescued by us from a humiliation of being unwanted (defeat at the polls) as we require a rescue by that leader who is to save us from our potential for humiliation. Here is our bilateral deficiency, ours as well as our leaders; here is our universal vulnerability, the self-esteem of humanity that is ever wide open to trauma! Here is the underlying core of man's imperfection, his Achilles' heel — his narcissism.

To love and to be loved requires an element of narcissism, an essence of self-love: but it also requires a mutuality of rescue of one creature by another. It seems we cannot love ourselves without being loved by another and we cannot love another without being loved by ourselves. It is this double equation that must be rescued in totality by the masses and their leader as they join in the mutuality of a charismatic political rescue operation.

I am aware that we who have special dependencies and vulnerabilities of self-esteem are most reluctant to have exposed the infantile rescue which we would psychologically perpetrate in liaison with our leader. It seems far more acceptable for us to disguise such residual vulnerabilities, both our own and those of our leader; such frailties, if acknowledged, would require then a further protection from the newly conscious and crushing feelings of impotence that would break through. For the sake of our self-esteem, we prefer instead to foster an illusion, one in which our hero is indeed an autonomous superman, a little damaged, as we see ourselves, but from a wound that he comes by valiantly, a wound emblematic of heroic front-line action as our personal representative in the 'big fight'. If by any chance our chosen hero should in fact be happily endowed with that extra x factor that allows him to actualize his heroics with personal acts of bravery, then so much more convincing is the aura of omnipotence that such a leader can cast over his people; all the more certainly does he become superman. Having wounds to show for his trouble is proof positive of both his own invincibility and that of the following who can identify with him.

Such a leader, approximating the hero lying dormant in the depths of our mass psyche, holds the key to unlock the encasement that confines all the charismatic delights of our earliest yearnings. It is he who holds the likelihood of helping us deny the biological clocks that ever whisper their 'demonic' message of an inexorable life with death; it is he above all whom we ordain to the task of triggering our need to subvert our own barrier of the will, toward a war against the uncanny. In so doing, it is he whom we see as helping us strengthen the sieve-like barrier of conscience that is our shield. Our rescue agent can overwhelm us in a double coup — one of simple idealization in the first instance, and one compounded with a rescue from mortality in the second. With the aggressions of our barrier of the will.displaced now onto an uncanny monster that must be destroyed, we are indeed wide open to the ultimate rescue — one that reaches down into the hypnoid strata of our minds, down further into *déjà-vu*, rekindling the animism and the magic of our childhood, re-igniting our personal family romance. Then as he penetrates deeper into the realm of all our subtleties of stigma, foreignness, and the 'primal scene' enigma, he finally recaptures the 'promised land' of our most infantile familiarities with the primal mother.

Chapter 7

Beyond charisma

According to the underlying logic of this thesis, from the moment a new leader of either type takes office, certain major forces in the psychology of the people are already at work undermining the leader's popularity and pressing for his eventual elimination from that office. Fortunately for a leader's future, the machinery of government and the laws dictating tenure of office aim to back up all the other more supporting forces whose interests are to maintain and preserve an unbroken term for the leader. Instabilities in office-holding for leaders have been more typical of dictatorships in some of the underdeveloped nations; though an exception in a more progressive democratic society was the chaotic period in France's post-war politics when leaderships changed hands in a matter of days.

When we examine the usual aftermath that follows the ascent of a new political figure to power in a democratic society, the fact that the laws are laid down to expedite his ability to lead does not mean that, from a psychological standpoint, the leader maintains a popular majority throughout his period of office. A recent example is of an American president psychologically destroyed as a leader long before the elective process inspired his easing himself from office. How does such a political demise of a leader take place? Some explain it by purely sociological factors, such as changes in the economy; a crisis or a lack of crisis, others point out, has much to do with stability in leadership. But to suggest that the only crucial mechanics in operation are sociological negates a deeper process that goes on in a people. It is another matter, of course, to try separating out and measuring this underlying psychological current of our attitudes towards leaders, especially when there is a major socio-economic upheaval. This in practice is an impossible task; all we can do really is acknowledge and identify the undercurrent for what it is.

In the pre-disenchantment stage of a child's imagery of his parents, while he is still captivated with the idealized omnipotence of his father for example, his interaction with his young peers on the street and in the school reflects a chauvinistic defence of the family colours that he genetically represents. As far as the youngster is concerned, his father is either stronger or wiser, or richer or braver, or kinder or harder-working than the father of his buddy. It is surprising how one's progeny manage to invent something of which they can be proud: their father can drink more, shout louder, or gamble more than their buddy's. If anyone really believes that people completely outgrow this process of primary idealization or, for that matter, surmount the subsequent phases of disenchantment which are always the aftermath of such idealization, then he is ignoring all the derivatives of the entire phenomenon as they show themselves, not only in the family romance of their later childhood, but more significantly in the communal romance of politics. Anyone who has observed or taken an active part in the kind of dialogue that commonly occurs between spokesmen for different nations will attest to this fact.

For example, not too long ago I was party to such a debate among a group of Canadian and American delegates to a psychiatric convention, and I can report on my own impassioned participation in this process whose undercurrents were of the same romantic quality as those of the child. In this particular engagement with my equally semi-inebriated colleagues from across the border, we were comparing our respective nation's leaders. Where on earlier occasions the argument had been about the President's muscles against the Prime Minister's sophistication, now the crux of the debating point was, which nation had the worst leader. In retrospect, the interesting part of such disputes is the way such discussions really screen out the source of the real complaints. On the surface, such arguments take the form of a political harangue on apparently rational sociological and economic issues; yet perhaps unconscious to most of us is the innate grudge we hold against our leaders — for their freedoms, their strengths, their power, and the obvious manner in which they continue to thrive both personally and communally on all those laurels that go with their office. We admire them and yet resent them for the lavish aristocratic protocol that takes them away from us commoners and propels them towards their own lofty world.

As we watch our leader hobnob with the leaders of the world's nations, we perceive a magnified replica of our original wandering parent, a repetition of the possessive child's early awareness of those socializations of his elders that left him completely excluded. As with our parents' public lives, where we observed activities that could only vaguely be applied to our personal benefit, so it is with the global excursions of our leaders, whose social lives only serve to remind us that they too are by no means our personal hand-servants and private companions. To our childhood minds, part of our life's plan orients around the concept that our parents will grow 'down' as we grow 'up'; later in our adult lives, as it relates to our leader, we learn otherwise: as we grow 'down', our leader grows 'up'!

Of course, there are many real issues for our discontent with leaderships: anxieties about selling wheat, evidence in the press of political mismanagement, unemployment and inflation — all such matters are rational concerns. The cry of youth is by no means a voice of pure oedipal defiance. 'Our nation is one of violence! The young are dying because of a nation's pride!' These are no mere neurotic carpings any more than are the laments of the businessmen for whom 'the bears have been howling for too long on Wall Street'. There are realities which not only leaders but all the citizenry of a nation have to deal with: yet, if the framework for these sober matters were not so permeated with the undercurrents of all those infantile elements of idealization and disenchantment which so typically provide a major core of the motivating force of political dissent, some of these more agonizing and confusing issues might in fact become more successfully resolved.

I have already described one group of the disenchanted — the anarchistic. Their psychic dynamisms, operating in many instances toward a position of triumph by attrition, would bring a doom to both the traditional great man as well as to the charismatic leader — a doom to all leaders in fact. All contestants for leadership, even on the very eve of their victory at the polls, are already on the way out, as far as the anarchistically disposed are concerned. If one listens to the quality of their disenchantments, it is difficult to distinguish them from the logical rationalism of that segment of the people more immediately concerned with the real socioeconomic issues. Complaining wheat farmers, industrialists, longshoremen, labour unionists, or members of the many professional societies are by no means devoid of these undercurrents of anarchistic brooding. The surface camouflage of such disenchantment looks quite rational: 'look at our leader, did he ever tell us what was really going on in Pakistan?' 'He is selling out Canada to the people across the border!' 'Where is his just society?' 'They say he's grown since he came to office; grown what — longer hair?'

Many of the complaints and the public disillusionments of people do revolve around kernels of truth about a charismatic leader's performance, but, perhaps at an unconscious level in many instances, these laments often come from people who bitterly sense the actual growth of their leader's psyche during his tenure of office. And why should his psyche not grow? The office is tailor-made for character development, carrying limitless possibilities for a heightening of a leader's stature. There have been few holding the highest office of their land who have not realized, during that period, a major expansion in all the dimensions of their personalities. But what about we the people who elected them? We claimed a charismatic leader as our proxy; he was to represent everything we could be and wanted to be. Yet in the aftermath of the election, in that sobering period following the elation and the mania, we become quickly dislodged of our festive mood; the intoxication of the romantic fantasy wears off; we are left with a stony reality of ourselves that compares unfavourably with our previous hopes for what the leader would bring to our lack-lustre lives.

The honeymoon is over much sooner for the people than for the leader. After a relatively comfortable period of 'connubial bliss', there has to come the recognition that we are not going to get what we hoped for after all. It is much the same with one's love life; after the initial phase of delight, even though there remains an intellectual awareness that one's love object is just as good if not a better person than before, most people do not remain as 'taken' with the same zest that they experienced a few years before. The undercurrents of rankling frustration and feeling left behind are complaints heard many times over from both lovers and political followers. There exists in people a desire to see themselves as always growing — rarely growing older or wiser but more commonly growing stronger and bigger and 'better' (whatever 'better' is). As with one's lover, so with one's leader: after a certain period of time, how much 'better' can we be with either? The day must come when the process of disenchantment and the feelings of being left behind creep in. But our leader grows bigger and stronger and healthier and richer and much more dignified. He becomes the epitome of the traditional patriarch!

We realize that we are growing 'down' and that all our dreams are fading of becoming a chief, of ending up free — free of the yoke of the 'great man', free to transcend group psychology, free to possess the primal mother all to ourselves. Instead, we are drained, and 'he' thrives! This man has got to go!

The disengagement of a people from its leader is a frightening yet fascinating phenomenon. The reactions of populations in the 1940s against their leaders — against Mussolini, against Hitler, even against Churchill who helped secure a victory for his people with freedom and dignity — these have been paralleled by more recent uprisings of public opinion against national heroes such as MacArthur, Stalin, and de Gaulle. In Canada, Pierre Trudeau acknowledged the process shortly after his own election in 1968, realizing that the mania surrounding his election was doomed to an inevitable aftermath of disenchantment; and it began immediately with cries that the country had been 'had'. The phenomenon of disillusion is just as much a part of the charismatic process as is the mania and the intoxication; both are the stuff of the people — an intrinsic sign of the cyclical moods and tastes of humanity. The cycle runs its historical course in repeating waves: first the hunger, then the satiation, then the disgruntlement, and then the hunger all over again — a cycle like a sequence of transient love affairs or the fickle dietary cravings of a pregnant woman.

The masses at large are as entitled to a change in their politics and their leader as they are to a new personal lifestyle. Obviously these changes in lifestyle dictate the elements which a public wishes to find in its leader, just as the style of a leader provokes its own inspirational effects on the deportment of a people. A population looking for a respite from a period of financial austerity will not surprisingly seek a leader whose image reflects festivity; the less obvious equation is when an inflationary economy provokes a qualm in the public that triggers a shift towards austerity. A similar reciprocal equation holds true for violence in the streets vis-à-vis law and order.

THE ILLUSORY ESCAPE FROM THE GROUP

Freud (1921) drew attention to the difference between a sexually oriented affair involving action and satiation and one of a more sensually inhibited nature, such as the enchantment with an object from a distance — a state that is familiar to all of us. Freud drew on this difference to explain how all political leaders in a group hold the potential for bonding the loyalties in their following, simply out of this very lack of complete gratification for the worshippers in relation to their leader. This idea, of course, is in direct sequel to his theory on the primal horde.

This volume has already made an alternate proposal to Freud's view on group psychology in emphasizing a more primary dynamism that operates in the deeper springs of public opinion relating to leadership. Especially in the kind of democracy that we have today, where patriarchy, mob psychology, and the coercive forces of tyranny are on the wane, we find ourselves with a model for group living that at least more closely approximates some kind of free society; our political affiliations and our options for leadership can be exercised in a more individualistic way. I have suggested that, if anything, the common bond in many present democratic societies has more the flavour of an identification of one individual with his fellow in terms of his more anarchistic ambitions for his own personal independence, a posture which in turn masks, yet reflects, his deeper yearning for the pivotal primal mother. It is logical to suggest, then, that out of such a futile endless drive for a satisfaction and a sole possession of this pivotal mother, comes man's anarchistic need to disengage himself from all leaders, no matter of what kind. Not so much from obedience to a primal horde structure that demands our toleration of the endless deprivation that leaderships in one form or another must impose for the common good, but rather from the endless sense of an inner quest for a reunion with the primal mother image, do we mobilize the zeal, especially at the stage of adolescent anarchism, to break the shackles obstructing us from an unconscious consummation with our first love. The closest we can come in reality to fulfilling such a love is in our personal sexual adaptation outside all groups, and free from the harness of a leader.

What if our leader were a pivotal mother, a beautiful and tender enchantress yearning to fulfil our group need? Would she enjoy the capacity to enlist a nation in a permanent human bondage? The answer is obviously 'no'. A total psychological satisfaction for the group is as hopeless an illusion, even with such a pivotal mother at the helm, as is charismatic imagery. The striving for self-fulfilment with such a leader may unquestionably be very much part of psychological reality: the actualization of the fulfilment is a fantasy without hope. Don Quixote's dream of reaching the unreachable star is the psychic wish of all mankind; but the star itself continues to escape us all.

There have been leaders who have held office for lengthy periods of time; could they not have remained in power till their death? It is my impression that a continuum in leadership stands opposed to anarchistic psychology, and that fear alone will account for any exceptional instances of prolonged tenure in leadership. Then again, leaders like Churchill and de Gaulle made comebacks which can only be explained as a response to crisis, in which libido and the quest for the pivotal mother gives way to a patriarchal rescue from the dangers without and within; aggression, not libido, becomes under these conditions the societal order of the day. In time of danger, whether from the elements, war, disease, or civil strife, libido gives ground; festivity and play defer to austerity, to self-sacrifice, and to the encroachments of law and order. The time of crisis brings on Freud's great man and all its group psychology of the primal horde.

THE INSIGHTFUL SOCIETY

Though this study has chosen to emphasize the role of the people in their capacity to anticipate and project an image of leadership that is appropriate for them in their times, I did say earlier that more often than not, in the evolution of a society, certain figures have emerged from the rank and file of humanity whose personality and character structure have not only suitably approximated the image of the people's choice but who by the structure of their own ideological positions have spearheaded the dreams of a nation, thereby making an indelible impact not only on the political forces of one nation but on the political complexion of the world at large. Though the psychology of political leaders will be investigated in depth in another volume, it is only appropriate to offer in this closing chapter some of the salient features common to leaders in general, especially to those of our particular times. In condensed form, a blueprint of such motivating psychology might serve as a tool in anticipating what we may expect in the immediate future of our national politics.

Everything that has been described as germane to the formation of an individual citizen's identity is, of course, equally applicable to the leader himself; after all, the leaders of the future, just as those of the past and of the present, will be and are but the products of our mass society. The leader brings with him to public office the same instinctual drives, the same hopes, ambitions, and frustrations that we, his following, experience. He brings with him into public life a similar assortment of conflicts from his own childhood; he has his own strata of infantile delights, he undergoes his struggles for an autonomy and for an emancipation from primal objects, he experiences the same tedious processes in ego-development with its idealizations and its disenchantments, and most certainly he feels some agonizing of a conscience that must adapt itself not only to his own individual psychology but to the group structure as well.

Our leader of today is burdened with the same libidinous forces as the rest of the nation he serves. Many of us, I suspect, carry over the infantile concept of a leader as celibate — a denial of the possibility that, as with monarchs of yore, libido for the leader is potentially more satiable than it is for the average citizen. Perhaps it is unrealistic for us not only to anticipate but to hope that the erotic instinct in our leader is harnessed by an ego of more robust fibre than our own, since it seems extremely doubtful in the face of the documentations of history that this is so. But one thing can be stated of leadership in general that is perhaps a tribute to the plasticity of the ego — that the office of top leadership itself holds the most likely promise of permitting an ego-identity that is more resolvedly developed than that of any other citizen in the land, and this despite the intense narcissism of political life with its matrix of omnipotence, with its oedipal contests, and its diplomatic intrigues that reflect all so clearly the underlying motivations that must have prompted so many leaders to choose such a calling. The need to be victor over the vanquished, to be a leader over a following, to be a ruler rather than to be ruled — these drives in political leaders are only topped in their intensity by the need of these same leaders to be loved by the people they serve.

The structure and development of conscience in political leaders is another matter entirely. We tread on a faulty premise when we ascribe to politicians a healthier, a more mature, and a less corruptible conscience than is possessed by the people they lead. One task of a leader should be suitably to represent the conscience of a people *en masse.* Group conscience has through the ages reflected a set of values that both quantitatively and qualitatively differ from the conscience that stems from our more individualized psychological development. In family life, people are reared from infancy within a framework that encompasses many golden rules; manipulation and deceit are frowned upon; taking advantage of one's neighbour is a vice; expediency, cunning, and the use of power and intrigue are to be deplored and shunned; aggression, bloodshed, and violence are against all laws; assassination, military coups, and the instigation of civil strife that aims to pit brother against brother or aims to fragment the solidarity of the state — these are punishable offences under the law. But few of these rules apply in group psychology, especially in time of national or international crisis. The leader of a nation is permitted a more flexible and more corruptible exercise in group conscience, where a rule that applies one day applies not at all the next. Group psychology in our contemporary times still adheres to a premise of conscience which both dictates and follows the archaic dictum that 'all is fair in love and war'. In the name of nationalism or internationalism, of good or welfare, or of patriotism, anything can be done; in international diplomacy 'games', an attack is labelled a defence, just as a defence is called an attack. All the rules that ordinarily apply to a citizen's private life are suspended within the chambers of the government, where the welfare of the nation is the business of the day.

Let us not confuse the voice of infantile disenchantment among people who look to downgrade all leadership and its governmental apparatus with those in our society who speak out boldly and actively as critics and watchdogs of both government and the people governed. There have been recently a number of cases involving the release of information classified as non-public by governments, and people are becoming aware of the leaks and the lies that may or may not emanate from high office. This extreme secretiveness had led to a cry from the people demanding the truth. The people of a democracy are entitled to know what their government is doing; this knowledge offers to a voting public the minimal power that is their right to possess as participants in representational government. Only a few years ago, media encroachments on government documents would have been considered practically acts of treason, but the public today is no longer the same naive and gullible mass of humanity. There is some evidence that people are no longer satisfied to remain sheep.

But democracy has still a long way to go. The machinery of the people's representation in government is still faulty: for example, the political process by which we choose our delegates and representatives is certainly worthy of overhaul. The complacent reassurances that ours is the best government in the world provide little cause for celebration. Efforts have been made to investigate the advantages and pitfalls in a more detailed screening of the personality characteristics of the various political figures who aspire to top leadership in a country. For the past decade, I have been one of a group which has been studying many volunteers from among leaders in Canadian politics to discover their psychological profiles. Like many others, I too once held that people were entitled to leaders not only in good physical health but free as well from any gross mental disorder. The purposes of this pursuit were neither wholly academic or scientific exploration nor simply the improvement the psycho-politics of our society. For I can not help harbouring qualms (which one spokesman of our nation's 'spiritual' media recently suggested was pure paranoia) lest a romantically inclined public figure with a 'cause' emerge upon the public scene, there to incite the kind of barbaric and savage racial hatreds that marked some of the dark days of recent history. The optimistic writings of Arthur Schlesinger Jr clearly infer that such a politics cannot take hold in a democratic society; but my own judgment is that in all likelihood it won't. My reservations derive from my views on group psychology. People have still some way to go before one can truly rest assured that we have arrived at a point where democracy can withstand all onslaughts.

The idea of some kind of board to screen all leadership candidates, at least for any possible evidence of incipient psychopathy or psychosis, can easily be attacked as a basic intrusion into the democratic process itself. Who would screen the screeners? But every nation has its cultural consensus on what constitutes mental health, and it is clearly desirable that a leader who aspires to represent the will of a nation should be mentally sound. It is equally clear that it is the people at large who should be the screeners, for we are our own experts when it comes to choosing our leaders. But for this we have to know about their mental and physical health as well as something of group psychology, and to be as fully aware as possible of the inner yearnings and perhaps hitherto unconscious projections which we employ in our political and electoral decisions. It is not mere rhetoric to say that democracy is the maturation and self-fulfilment of the individual; and the individual, in democratic theory, cannot abdicate this responsibility for himself. Each has the obligation to serve not only himself, but his leaders and his society as well — to exercise a responsible and knowledgeable citizenship by engaging in active political discussion and correspondence, by contributing toward public opinion, and, most importantly, by the casting of a responsible ballot.

As I have tried to show, everyone has a psyche with striking similarities to his fellows'; herein lies the basis for group psychology. And in any psychology of groups, there is always the potential for mass behaviour, whether such be induced in us as consumers by the modern media or as the designers of leadership under the stimulation of political manipulators. If we acknowledge the force behind these facts of communal life, then we owe ourselves and each other the protection that comes from an awareness of the psychological seductions offered us by leaders and their image makers, as well as those that come from the infectious suggestibility of the group.

Burdensome as these obligations are, the solution of an escape from the group is hardly feasible. Both the 'massists' and the 'anti-massists' are motivated by the same dynamism that has always inspired humanity — the search for the possession of the primal mother. By refusing to relinquish this quest whilst claiming to have escaped from the group, the anti-massist cherishes a 'freedom' that is nothing more than illusion; for as Durkheim has observed, the soul of mankind (ego ideal) can only receive its spark from those who reach out to confirm their group fellows' callings (group conscience). By the confirmation of ideals, I do not suggest some indiscriminate sharing by individuals of the ideals of the largest and most powerful group: what is meant is that each individual should be prepared to embrace or to challenge (and be challenged by) those group ideals that provoke either his individual endorsement or dissension. Rather than priding ourselves on some illusory escape from the group, we serve each other far more by the understanding of our ways within the politics of the group.

Earlier, I stated that it was my aim to offer some insights into the ways we, the people, exercise our personal options in our choice of national leaders. Toward this end, I have attempted to bring into focus those features of our individual development, that when gathered together under the umbrella of our group psychology, come to represent a significant undercurrent in the mainstream operations of the mass psyche. The emphasis has particularly dwelt on the inherent need in mankind for a rescue of its narcissism, a salvage of the early heroic ideals that give content to both our personal and communal family romance. I have tried to reveal the deeper roots of certain forces that pit man against man in an anarchistic struggle to gain the tools and the power to win a way back to the possession of the primal pivotal mother — an immortality so to speak, aimed at offsetting the inexorable biological signals that carry us along the one-way trip through the obstacles of the uncanny, toward our ultimate fate. I have offered an inventory of those ingredients of our individual and mass psyche that go into the development of conscience, and into the barrier of the will, which, vulnerable as it is, stands potentially corruptible by the demon called fear that lurks inside all of us. Finally I have tried to dramatize mankind's consistent recoil from living with the knowledge of death, a recoil that may produce a subversion of the will, sometimes in the form of a charismatic rescue operation that heightens the intensity of the idealizations that we unconsciously project onto an outside heroic agent. I hope that readers may have come to know more of these inner and outer forces that can threaten to deprive us of our judgment and our will.

References

Balint, Michael, 1960. Primary narcissism and primary love, *Psychoanaltyic Quarterly* 29: 6-43

Berelson, B. R., Lazarsfeld, P. F., McPhee, W. N. 1954. *Voting* (University of Chicago Press)

Brown, Norman O., 1959. *Life against Death* (Wesleyan University Press), 100-9

Deutsch, Felix, 1959. *On the Mysterious Leap from the Mind to the Body* (International Universities Press), 59-97

Deutsch, Helene, 1945. *The Psychology of Women* (Grune and Stratton), 426-7

Durkheim, Emile, 1915. *The Elementary Forms of Religious Life* (Allen & Unwin, 5th ed., 1964), 36-8, 262-72

Erikson, Erik H., 1968. *Identity, Youth, and Crises* (W. W. Norton), 258-9

Feuer, Lewis, 1969. *The Conflict of Generations* (Basic Books), 54-166

Frazer, Sir James, 1890. *The New Golden Bough*, ed. Theodor Gaster (Criterion Books, 1959), 165, 217

Freud, Anna, 1946. *The Ego and Mechanisms of Defense* (International Universities Press), 57, 128

Freud, Sigmund, 1895. *Project for a Scientific Psychology*, Standard ed., I (Hogarth, 1966), 332-5

- 1913. *Totem and Taboo*, Standard ed., XIII (Hogarth, 1962) 1-162

- 1919. *The Uncanny*, Standard ed., XVII (Hogarth, 1962), 218-52

- 1921. *Group Psychology and the Analysis of the Ego*, Standard ed., XIII (Hogarth, 1962), 111-28

- 1939. *Moses and Monotheism*, Standard ed., XXIII (Hogarth, 1962), 7-137

Gill, Merton M., and Brennan, Margaret, 1959. *Hypnosis and Related States* (International Universities Press)

Graves, Robert, 1948. *The White Goddess*, 3rd amended ed. (Faber, 1959), 323-32, 466-78

Harlow, H. F., 1962. The effects of early experience upon the personal, social, heterosexual, and maternal behavior of Rhesus monkeys, *Transactions of the American Neurological Association* 87: 9

- and Zimmerman, R. R., 1959. Affectional response in the infant monkey, *Science* 130: 421-32

Hibbert, Christopher, 1962. *Il Duce: The Life of Benito Mussolini* (Longmans), 15-16

Klein, Melanie, 1932. *Psychoanalysis of Children* (Hogarth, 1937), 245-8

Kohut, Heinz, 1971. *The Analysis of the Self* (International Universities Press), 212-13

Lane, Robert, 1959. *Political Life* (The Free Press), 119

Lasswell, Harold, 1930. *Psychopathology and Politics* (Viking Press), 78-126

Mahler, Margaret, 1967. On human symbiosis and the vicissitudes of individuation, *Journal of the American Psychoanalytic Association* 15, 4: 74-63

Niebuhr, R., and Sigmund, P., 1969. *The Democratic Experience* (Praeger), 24

Parsons, Talcott, 1967. *Sociological Theory and Modern Society* (The Free Press), 93-8, 223-59, 370

Rank, Otto, 1914. The myth of the birth of the hero, *Nervous and Mental Diseases* monograph 18

Roazen, Paul, 1968. *Freud: Political and Social Thought* (Alfred Knopf), 167-92

Róheim, Géza, 1943. The origin and function of culture, *Nervous and Mental Diseases* monograph 69: 74-84

Schiffer, Irvine, 1959. Psychoanalytic observations on the mechanism of conversion symptoms. *Psychoanalytic Review* (1964) V, 2: 33-42

– 1962. The psychoanalytic study of the development of a conversion symptom, *International Journal of Psychoanalysis* 43: 169-74

Schilder, Paul, 1953. *Medical Psychology* (International Universities Press), 261-4

Schlesinger, Arthur Jr, 1960. On heroic leadership, from *The Politics of Hope* (Houghton Mifflin, 1963), 3-22

Spitz, René A., 1950. *The Psychoanalytic Study of the Child*, V, *Relevancy of Direct Intent Observation* (International Universities Press), 66-73

Velikovsky, Immanuel, 1955. *Earth in Upheaval* (Doubleday), 108-53

Weber, Max, 1922. *The Sociology of Religion* (Beacon Press, 1963), 2-3, 46-59, 149-57